'Written in an electrified poetic style that glitters and shivers and is drenched in intelligent and stimulating allusions, and peppered with striking images and insights, the new book by Antonino Ferro and Giuseppe Civitarese is nothing if not exciting and thought-provoking. The book conveys the liveliness and playfulness of the authors' approach to contemporary psychoanalysis and bravely presents challenges and reassessments of nuclear theoretical concepts. *Playing and Vitality in Psychoanalysis* crackles and sizzles and might well shake psychoanalysis to its very core. It is a rivetingly smart book.'

Elias M. da Rocha Barros *is a training analyst at the Brazilian Psychoanalytical Society of São Paulo and distinguished fellow of the British Psychoanalytical Society and Institute*

'*Playing and Vitality in Psychoanalysis* is about field theory, but more importantly it is field theory – overbrimming with the characters and the stories and the plots and the angst and the pleasure – all of which is brought to life by a clarity of thinking that is rare in psychoanalysis today. One cannot read this book without being changed by it personally and professionally.'

Thomas Ogden *most recently authored* Coming to Life in the Consulting Room (*Routledge, 2021*)

'Antonino Ferro and Giuseppe Civitarese, playfully and with great vitality, lead us through the intimacy of their clinical practice. Through the numerous characters that circulate through the book, Ferro and Civitarese offer us a psychoanalytic reflection from a true aesthetic experience resulting from the very reading of the text. Several of Bion's and many other authors' ideas, such as the concept of the analytic field, come to life and are illustrated and deepened through the many clinical situations presented and through the authors' original reflections. Reading this book will certainly be a pleasant experience of pleasure, discovery, learning and enchantment.'

Ruggero Levy *is a member of the SPPA, Porto Alegre, Brazil*

Playing and Vitality in Psychoanalysis

Building on their long-lasting scientific partnership, Civitarese and Ferro offer an array of thought-provoking writings bolstered by extensive clinical material, attesting to their shared interpretation of psychoanalysis not only as a treatment for psychic suffering but also as inherently pleasurable and vitalizing.

In chapters that reflect inclinations, fantasies and obsessions that are both shared and personal, and by engaging with topics various enough to include dreams, ethics, emotions and aesthetics, the authors demonstrate how the practice of psychoanalysis might no longer be an insidiously moralistic or ideological exercise but rather a practice aimed at opening up and liberating the mind. By providing detailed engagement with the work of Bion and Ogden, as well as insights from their own substantial expertise, the authors explore how the synonymous concepts of playing and vitality can meaningfully inform and change clinical psychoanalytic practice.

With rich clinical material and a strong foundation in established theory, this book will appeal to psychoanalysts, psychoanalytic therapists and postgraduate students hoping to make more room in the psychoanalytic lexicon for words like pleasure, dreaming, creativity, hospitality and growth.

Giuseppe Civitarese is a psychiatrist and training and supervising analyst of the Italian Psychoanalytic Society (SPI) and a member of the American Psychoanalytic Association. He lives and is in private practice in Pavia, Italy. He is the editor of the *Rivista di Psicoanalisi*, the official journal of the SPI.

Antonino Ferro is a psychiatrist and training and supervising analyst in the Italian Psychoanalytic Society, of which he was President, and a member of the American Psychoanalytic Association and the International Psychoanalytical Association. He has been a visiting professor of psychoanalysis in various institutions in Europe, North America, South America and Australia. He received the Sigourney Award in 2007.

Psychoanalytic Field Theory Book Series

S. Montana Katz & Giuseppe Civitarese
Series Editors

The *Psychoanalytic Field Theory Book Series* was initiated in 2015 as a new subseries of the *Psychoanalytic Inquiry Book Series*. The series publishes books on subjects relevant to the continuing development of psychoanalytic field theory. The emphasis of this series is on contemporary work that includes a vision of the future for psychoanalytic field theory.

Since the middle of the twentieth century, forms of psychoanalytic field theory emerged in different geographic parts of the world with different objectives, heuristic principles, and clinical techniques. Taken together they form a family of psychoanalytic perspectives that employs a concept of a bi-personal psychoanalytic field. The *Psychoanalytic Field Theory Book Series* seeks to represent this pluralism in its publications. Books on field theory in all its diverse forms are of interest in this series. Both theoretical works and discussions of clinical technique will be published in this series.

The series editors are especially interested in selecting manuscripts which actively promote the understanding and further expansion of psychoanalytic field theory. Part of the mission of the series is to foster communication amongst psychoanalysts working in different models, in different languages, and in different parts of the world. A full list of titles in this series is available at: www.routledge.com/Psychoanalytic-Field-Theory-Book-Series/book-series/FIELDTHEORY

Playing and Vitality in Psychoanalysis

Giuseppe Civitarese and Antonino Ferro

Translated by Ian Harvey

Routledge
Taylor & Francis Group

LONDON AND NEW YORK

Cover image: Drawing by Rocco Civitarese

First published in English 2022
by Routledge
4 Park Square, Milton Park, Abingdon, Oxon OX14 4RN

and by Routledge
605 Third Avenue, New York, NY 10158

Routledge is an imprint of the Taylor & Francis Group, an informa business

© 2022 Giuseppe Civitarese and Antonino Ferro

Translated by Ian Harvey

Published in Italian by Cortina Raffaello 2020

The right of Giuseppe Civitarese and Antonino Ferro to be identified as authors of this work has been asserted in accordance with sections 77 and 78 of the Copyright, Designs and Patents Act 1988.

British Library Cataloguing-in-Publication Data
A catalogue record for this book is available from the British Library

Library of Congress Cataloging-in-Publication Data
Names: Civitarese, Giuseppe, 1958– author. | Ferro, Antonino,
    1947– author. | Harvey, Ian, active 2013, translator.
Title: Playing and vitality in psychoanalysis / Giuseppe Civitarese
    and Antonino Ferro ; translated by Ian Harvey.
Other titles: Vitalità e gioco in psicoanalisi. English
Identifiers: LCCN 2021061915 (print) | LCCN 2021061916 (ebook) |
    ISBN 9781032245041 (hardback) | ISBN 9781032245058
    (paperback) | ISBN 9781003279020 (ebook)
Subjects: LCSH: Psychoanalysis. | Play—Psychological aspects. |
    Vitality—Psychological aspects.
Classification: LCC BF173 .C496513 2022 (print) | LCC BF173
    (ebook) | DDC 150.19/5—dc23/eng/20220105
LC record available at https://lccn.loc.gov/2021061915
LC ebook record available at https://lccn.loc.gov/2021061916

ISBN: 978-1-032-24504-1 (hbk)
ISBN: 978-1-032-24505-8 (pbk)
ISBN: 978-1-003-27902-0 (ebk)

DOI: 10.4324/9781003279020

Typeset in Times New Roman
by Apex CoVantage, LLC

Contents

Preface

Playing and Vitality in Psychoanalysis is but one further stage in a decades-long scientific partnership whose most recent publications have been *The Analytic Field* (2015) and *A Short Invitation to Psychoanalysis* (2018). With the exception of the two chapters on Ogden and on the correspondence between Bion and Rickman, all the chapters in this book present extensive clinical material. This testifies to a strong interpretation of psychoanalysis understood as a treatment for psychic suffering. The various essays reflect inclinations, fantasies and obsessions that are both shared and personal. To make the reading experience more varied, our respective contributions alternate in the book. At times the tone is closer to the spoken language, and we hope this will render the text immediate, spontaneous, "poetic", vital, playful; elsewhere it is more essayistic. We like to think that the parts that are more conversational provide a kind of connective tissue in which the more "academic" parts are "suspended". One can also imagine the book as a voyage through an archipelago with various stopovers to explore a succession of small islands. In this way – as always in our books – the reader will encounter a plethora of characters, stories, emotions, metamorphoses, insights. An array of characters will come on stage one after the other: a hound that turns into a chihuahua, an Oblomov armchair, the "pampering" field, an Id(e)a, a "destormed" storm, a masked TI – one thinks of Mandrake – a "pepper" fact, an "aubergine" fact, a "celery" fact, a Serb in a harem, pinkification, raw beta and cooked alpha, Botticelli's Primavera or Gilda in Charles Vidor's *noir* (in its "skeletonized" version), a horizontal 8, a U-turn, a wolf-woman, a pink bison, a hieroglyph mother, a transvestite, Locke(d), etc.

Permit us to express a small note of quiet satisfaction. Objective acknowledgements of the value of analytic field theory are growing steadily, as evidenced by the number of citations and the popularity index collated by Psychoanalytic Electronic Publishing, the largest international database of psychoanalytic literature. For example, for the whole of 2018 our work on metaphor was the most cited after Bion's *Attacks on Linking* if measured over the last five years, and seventh over the last decade; a few months later another work on transformation in hallucinosis (GC) was ranked fifth, also over the previous five-year period; and an article on transformation into dreams (AF) was third out of ten and ninth out of twenty, and so on. Albeit with some critical observations, a few years ago Kernberg already identified the analytic field theory of the so-called Italian post-Bionians as one of the main currents of contemporary psychoanalysis. Further authoritative confirmation has recently been added. In his *The Development of Relations*, Seligman (2016) drew up a chart in which we find contemporary Freudians, Kleinians and relationalists, followed by the authors of analytic field theory. Essentially, this means the Pavia School, but whose roots lie in terrain cultivated in Palermo by Francesco Corrao, in Rome by Claudio Neri, in Milan by Eugenio Gaburri and Luciana Nissim Momigliano, as well as by many others. Analytic field theory now dialogues with a great number of habitual interlocutors: Thomas Ogden, Lewis Aron, Jessica Benjamin, Jay Greenberg, Donnel Stern, Adienne Harris, Howard Levine, Larry Brown, Andrea Celenza, Joseph Aguayo, Avner Bergstein, etc. We point this out not because we wish to rest on our laurels – which, if anything, would be a sign of crisis – but to stimulate in our younger colleagues a passion for psychoanalysis that no longer has to look abroad. We are happy that for the first time Italian psychoanalysis features in the family photo – and indeed in the front row. We are thinking here of the symbolic value of certain historic photographs of groups of analysts gathered around Freud or Melanie Klein.

The idea we have of psychoanalysis is of something noble – a complex, non-reductionist discipline which has developed a method that has its own intrinsic beauty. As does literature, and as happens only to philosophy, in the best cases and thanks to its "specific" method – the Freudian *Junktim* of theory and empirical research – it can aspire to saying something unique and true about the essence of what constitutes the human dimension – a dimension which, however, gets lost when psychoanalysis becomes a kind of glass bead game. This often happens with metapsychology, and in this respect French psychoanalysis has been trend-setting; it reaches even grotesque proportions with Ego Psychology, also reappearing in those contemporary followers of Bion who are devotees of his abstraction and obscurity. There is also another way of dehumanizing psychoanalysis. This is what Bion alludes to in *Second Thoughts*, when he writes that sometimes the analyst's "qualification is an ability, thanks to projective identification (in which he does not believe), to preen himself on freedom from the psychosis for which he looks down upon his patients and colleagues" (1967, p. 162).

Bion spent much of his life as a scholar struggling against the insidious manner in which moralism (which has to do not with what is true but with the idea that one has of what is good or evil) dresses itself up as science. It is our hope that the practice of psychoanalysis will no longer be, as often happens despite its best intentions, an insidiously moralistic or ideological exercise. Rather, its aim should be to open up and liberate the mind. To achieve this, and without slipping into naivety, it must stop being "suspicious" in Ricoeur's sense of the word, in other words, it must stop "looking down" its nose. We are not talking about the personal qualities of the analyst but about a certain superegoic attitude that is intrinsic to Freud's theory of the demonic unconscious, and consequently to the stereotypical figure of the patient who resists, attacks, misunderstands, etc. It is thus imperative that we bring up to date the theoretical and technical tools of psychoanalysis in an authentically intersubjective sense. It is time to make more room in its lexicon for words like pleasure, dream, creativity, hospitality and growth – and for this reason our title invokes the "synonymous" concepts of vitality and playing.

Chapter 1

Dreams, transformations, deconstructions

A patient is attending four sessions of analysis a week. This information is important because it tells us about the degree of deconstruction that is possible. At the Wednesday session she describes how as a child she used to find it distressing to come home from school in the afternoon uncertain whether her mother would be there to open the front door when she knocked. Sometimes nobody would answer, which meant that, anxious because her mother was not there, she would have to go downstairs to the concierge's small flat where she would wait until her mother arrived. Sometimes her mother would get there fairly soon, but more often she would have to wait a long time. Once she even had to have dinner there.

Naturally, various listening perspectives are possible:

a) *(Hi)story*. On a concrete historical timeline that helps us carry out a survey on the patient's emotional life, this communication will take us along a path of reconstruction.

b) *Internal world*. An alternative approach would view the communication as something that concerns the internal object (mother) and the internal support object (the concierge). The former is relatively reliable but sometimes merges into an object that exposes her to a fear of abandonment; all this can come to life in a description of the patient's object "phantasies".

c) *Relationship*. With different shades of meaning, the communication could also be seen as the description the patient gives of the theme of "finding each other again" in the interval between sessions, the periods of waiting and the interplay between separation, encounters and further periods of waiting within the current relationship. It could be understood as a description of the patient's relationship with the analyst and the analyst's varying degrees of presence and absence; as the

DOI: 10.4324/9781003279020-1

result of the patient's capacity to monitor acceptance and rejection depending on the analyst's permeability *vis-à-vis* the multiple game of projective identifications; and also as a tool to measure the different degrees of being within a network – a sort of relational "4G" tester.

d) *Opening up resonating dream worlds and complex fields.* I would also argue that a fourth mode of listening is possible, one that is not interpretative but is a way of starting off the game. It is similar to bidding in bridge: I open with this bid,[1] what will you and the other "speakers" or characters of the field say [or what will *you* plural say] or what will they reply [or *you* plural reply]? What kind of game will come to life? What other bids will be made and how will the game develop further? And what is there to stop the game from being interrupted by all kinds of unexpected and unpredictable "arrivals" on the scene? These could range from unexpected "bids" or "declarations" to disruptions in the atmospheric conditions of the game owing to the arrival of "robbers" or the invasion of "aliens". How would the statements made by C (character) be perceived?

My argument so far is possible due to the varying degree of deconstruction and re-dreaming – the two instruments that create every possible transformation.

Of course, my way of thinking also rests on and has its roots in what we might call a "post-Bionian field" model of the mind.

Bionian and post-Bionian transformations

I use the term "transformations" in a very broad sense; I am thinking of the transformations from beta elements to alpha elements. I have dealt with this subject in many of my previous works; my aim here is to summarize and clarify systematically the key concepts that today fall under the term Bionian Field Theory.

Again, taken broadly we also have *narrative transformations*, which imply a different way of understanding the container – not so much as a spatial or volumetric container but rather as a container that develops within the narrative. A Jack the Ripper that roams the streets of London alone will be much more dangerous than one who is linked up with *Django Unchained*.

If both were then connected to Donald Duck, the danger level would sink even further. The narrative itself would be able to contain emotions that otherwise, if they were free, would come to resemble tsunamis.

I would now like to extrapolate the concepts Bion brings into focus in his *Transformations* (1965) by describing their applications from the point of view of the operations performed by the analyst in the session. The analyst might work in the field of *rigid-motion transformations*, that is, transformations where the initial figure is easily recognizable thanks to its significant level of invariance. These are what are observed when we interpret some of the patient's communications as transference.

In my opinion, operations like these can be very useful to the analyst as they have the potential to generate a basic level of relationality that can be seen as comparable to the trapeze artist's safety net.

The analyst operates differently when dealing with projective transformations than with rigid-motion transformations.

Here we find less invariance, and the transformations are not as easy to recognize. They are often generated by reverie, by the presentation of new facets of meaning and have their origin in an operational field model rather than in a theory.

In Bion's famous example, the patient says "ice-cream", but he interprets the "coldness" as containing the violent emotions of "I scream" (Bion, 1970).

Transformations in K are those that entail a bond of knowledge but do not produce any catastrophic changes – although they may at times pave the way for such changes: "Transformations in K are feared when they threaten the emergence of transformations in O" (Bion, 1965, p. 158). *Transformations in O* and catastrophic changes involve a sudden leap in mental development, which is achieved by way of a crisis that may at times even entail short periods of depersonalization.

Characteristic features of catastrophic change are violence and subversion of the system; and, for the analyst, awareness of feeling unable to spare themselves or their patient from an experience of "catastrophic" truth. As Bion states: "Transformations in O contrast with other transformations in that the former are related to growth in becoming and the latter to growth in 'knowing about' growth" (*ibid.*, p. 156). Resistance to an interpretation is therefore resistance to the passage from K to O. Such a change is "of particular concern to the analyst in his function of aiding maturation of the personalities of his patients" (*ibid.*, p. 158).

I leave aside *transformations in hallucinosis* (on this, see Civitarese's rich monograph, 2015), where the analyst might project theories onto the patient and then see them confirmed by evidence coming from the patient's clinical material.

Also worth recalling is Grotstein's brilliant insight that O needs to move through column 2 (the column of lies and dreams) in order to become understandable, thus building a daring bridge between dream and lie.

Transformations into dreams

Rotten fruit

I first began to think about the concept of *transformations into dreams* after hearing a French colleague describe an episode that he claimed had involved Freud. In one session, a patient had complained to Freud about his (the patient's) wife. He had spoken of how annoyed and frustrated he had felt listening to her complaints about the overripe fruit she had bought at the market. After a while, according to my French colleague, Freud had said: *"That's enough talk about fruit; it's time to turn inwards towards your emotion"*.

With this story in mind, finding himself with a patient who was complaining about something that was part of his external reality, my colleague told him: "Let's leave these things aside; why don't you try to look inside yourself".

The patient spent the rest of the session in absolute silence.

This was how I began to reflect on the concept of transformations into dreams, or rather, I began to think about what might happen if we were to adopt a sort of magical filter while listening to the communications coming from the patient; if, for example, the patient's communication, "My wife complained about rotten fruit . . ." were preceded by the filter "I dreamed that my wife was complaining about rotten fruit", then everything would change.

This would open the way for a communication that could convey multiple different meanings. Perhaps the most obvious meaning is that one aspect of the patient (the wife) is unhappy about receiving such poor-quality fruit from the greengrocer (the analyst), and rotten and indigestible interpretations (pears, apples).

Listening to each communication as though it were preceded by "I dreamed that . . ." opens up the analyst's mind to an infinite range of possible narrative developments.

Transformations into play

The concept of transformations in play first came to me while I was supervising a case.

Paper planes

An experienced analyst recounted a session with a young boy of about 7. The boy had started making paper planes and throwing them at her. When one struck her painfully in the corner of her eye, the normally very composed analyst got angry and started making and throwing paper planes back at him. But when one ended up hitting the boy in the eye, she quickly stopped and began to ask herself what on earth she was doing. She soon regained her composure, but by then the boy had started cursing and swearing at her.

To her bemusement, she found herself turning all these swear words into jocular rhyming verses. The boy would rail against her and she would convert his words into rhymes. Gradually the boy's anger subsided, and he invited her to have a go at swearing too. Perhaps still flushed by her previous anger, this came very easy to her and she let out a string of insults that the boy then turned into rhymes of his own.

The paper plane game thus turned into a kind of rhyming contest: they had stopped shooting arrows at each other and set about doing something they could both enjoy.

At the end of the session and for the first time, the boy said he couldn't wait to come back again. Over the next few sessions, they continued this game, with one swearing and the other transforming the swear words into extempore rhymes. The analyst came up with progressively more interpretative rhymes such as "The little son of a . . . was angry because . . .".

Another example of transformations into play

What I am about to describe was one of the most unusual situations I ever found myself in as an analyst. I had a patient who had been coming for four sessions a week but had never agreed to go on the couch. For a long time, her sessions were face to face until I began to realize how difficult it was to work properly under her controlling gaze.

I asked her if I could move my chair so that my back was turned towards her. She agreed because what was important to her was being able to keep an eye on me. After working like this for some time, the patient described *a dream in which she was about to move house*. Obviously, this gave me the opportunity to start discussing the subject of switching from two chairs to the standard analytic set-up of couch and chair.

Finally, she acquiesced and we agreed to make the change the following Monday. The fateful day arrived, but instead of heading to the couch, the patient quickly sat down in my chair! At that moment I had to make a split-second decision and abandon all possible interpretations. I simply went to the now empty couch and lay down. I took some slight comfort in remembering that when Marie Bonaparte began to suffer from particularly painful rheumatism, she would lie down on the couch while the patient would occupy the less comfortable chair.

My patient and I continued like this for some weeks, during which time I discovered that being an analyst on the couch did not cost me my role as "captain of the ship".

Needless to say, I tried to explore and interpret the situation, which continued unchanged until she told me about a secretary at her workplace who had taken over someone else's office and how she (of all people) had had to broach the subject with the secretary to fix things so that everyone could return to their rightful place. Naturally I took the opportunity to talk about this secretary and this was the first step towards our being able to plan a further move.

So eventually we both adopted our correct positions and the analytic journey continued in a more usual way. This "fact", I believe, represented the transformation into play of something that was not yet ready to be said, understood or rationalized, or which happened for reasons that were not yet clear.

Understanding this "fact" and being able to play with our "reciprocal workstations" enabled us to work fruitfully. Transformation into play made possible a metabolization and transformation of the patient's persecutory anxieties.

Note

1 In Italian "bid" is "dichiarazione", which is also used in expressions like "love declaration".

References

Bion, W.R. (1965). *Transformations: Change from Learning to Growth*. London: Heinemann.

Civitarese, G. (2015). Transformations in hallucinosis and the receptivity of the analyst. *International Journal of Psychoanalysis*, 96:1091–1116.

Chapter II

Vitality as a theoretical and technical parameter in psychoanalysis

If we read what Premoli's *Nomenclature Dictionary* (1913) says about the term "authenticity", we see it is defined as "giving authenticity" or "rendering authentic" an "act" or "document" so as to make it legally valid. The etymology of the word emphasizes the concept of authority as belonging to the person who acts as himself or herself. Two essential elements are therefore the notion of *agency* and respect for the law. The two things are in a relationship of co-implication: authority – which we could translate: the subject as the outcome of a process of individuation or personalization – emanates from respect for the law, from *common sense*. Close relatives of authenticity are "truth" and "vitality". We all use these terms in psychoanalysis and give them significant importance. All models of psychoanalysis put the concept of truth at the centre (Civitarese, 2014, 2018). However, these terms suffer from a singular lack of precision. The reason is soon exposed: it is because they have to do with the sphere of affection and sentiment, and therefore cannot be thematized. How one feels, whether vital or not, authentic (true) or not, cannot be reduced to a conceptual formula.

The scarf-serpent

A few years ago I described in a vignette an episode in which a visual image had shaken me out of a situation of mortiferous repetition with a patient with severe autistic traits and had, perhaps for the first time, made me feel a sense of vitality – an emotion that inevitably and usefully revitalized the relationship itself and the other, if only for what rational and emotional understanding was brought and especially because it renewed interest in a situation otherwise experienced as desperate. It so happened that, at the end of the session, my young patient had let her long scarf slip

DOI: 10.4324/9781003279020-2

a couple of times while wrapping it around her neck, and I had "seen" the snake that held her in an implacable grip, an image of the sternly obsessive thought that constricted her creativity. Then the image was immediately transformed by association into that of Ka, the snake from the *Jungle Book*, thus opening up scenarios that were both Oedipal (the snake of Eden) and playful.

So why is image so important in psychoanalysis? For one thing, because thought is eminently visual (as we know, *theoréin* means "to see"), but also because it is more ambiguous, more unstable, closer to the body and its emotional experiences than linguistic meanings. Even if still within the basic framework of humanity – that is of language as the only factor that allows us to access, as we say, the register of the symbolic, in other words, to gain self-awareness, to be able to say "I" or to think thoughts – images convey the knowledge of the body that is organized by rhythms and spacings that cannot be translated into words but which are no less important than words. The way to articulate these two dimensions of subjectivity is to think of chiasmus, the rhetorical figure used by Merleau-Ponty as an essential interweaving, a system of cross-references (Merleau-Ponty, 1945).

It goes without saying that images constitute the dream text, which we see more and more, to use a metaphor of Freud, as a poem of the mind; the poem of the mind that, when we are not too cluttered with violent emotions, helps us give a personal meaning (but one which is also impersonal or shared, consensual) to experience. Following some ideas I find are suggested by speculative thinking, I see the faculty of imagination as a kind of elf that revolves around the object to be known, no matter what it is, and that looks at it from many different perspectives; as it were, it takes many photographs. We feel true and real (authentic) not when we only have one picture of an object, as science seeks to provide us with, but when multiple images simultaneously give us back – as is the way of art – the truth of experience.

Talking bags

A second example I can give is from another essay published some years ago in which I described a very problematic situation – a patient who was not obsessive, like the one I mentioned, and whom I saw face to face weekly. She remained silent all the time. I drew on some images on the bags she carried with her and placed at her feet, which had made an impression on me: two small pumas, as in the logo of a well-known brand of shoes (were these scraps of aggression? I had asked myself, but they were also finally something alive), then two cartoon-style kittens (cuddles, tenderness). This is where my mental "photographs" followed: an empty pool, which one did not dare enter, sharks, coral reefs . . . and so on. We had managed to get characters into a play that at first seemed written by Beckett: this was a thought I had at the time and whose positive value I immediately felt, because I love Beckett's theatre. Then there were other characters with whom to construct, little by little, a story of the conscious and unconscious emotions that we experienced at every session.

Spacing 12

Oftentimes that which makes us experience a sense of authenticity and vitality is something that imposes itself because of its particular sensory impact. Suddenly I notice, when I am already immersed in a whole series of stories of a patient and the analyst, that, having reformatted the text of the protocol of a session described during a supervision, two lines of text have been lost at the foot of each page and that three or four times the computer used line spacing not of one or two but of 12! Of course, even though the computer belongs to an analyst and has "written" many texts on psychoanalysis, it cannot be said to have engaged in unconscious thinking, but a posteriori *our* unconscious cannot but re-signify any event from its own point of view. In short, the empty space immediately suggests to me that, despite a whole number of positive things, a void, an unbridgeable distance, seems to have been created between analyst and patient, that too many pieces of "text" are lost, and so on. Every time something like this happens, I feel gratitude for the analytic method and its intrinsic beauty. One of the recurrent thoughts I have at times is a sense of pity that every-thing we have said will be lost. Certain wonderful dreamlike constructions or puns: we talk about places in Sardinia and in a completely unexpected way Orosei is recast by a patient of mine as "you are gold" ("*sei oro*"); or, on another occasion "standby" becomes "stand by me", etc. Other times it can be a certain use of punctuation, or the hallucinosis of attributing a remark to the wrong character, and so on.

In contemporary psychoanalysis, this ability to give form to emotions has become the heart of treatment. It is even said that the mother loves the child through her capacity for reverie. If there is a bond of love, she is able to dream, that is to say, to intuit, the child's deep needs and anxieties and to contain them. In this way, by absorbing this transformational function, the mind settles in the body for the first time. As we can see, this is not a purely rational, but rather a rational, imaginative and affective process. Not only does that which philosophers call intentionality of act intervene, but also body intentionality. We could define it as pre-reflexive, even if, as already stated, it was already rooted in the symbolic. According to Bion, it is essential that analysts are able to be painters or photographers of emotions, which light up in the relationship or in the analytic field. Of course, this should not remain a vague and imprecise reference. If it did, it would not have much value. For an analyst, being an artist means having a rigorous theoretical framework and a coherent technique that allows the individual to make disciplined use of intuitive moments. The analyst's tool becomes the faculty of imagination, and since it is assumed that unconscious communication between minds is always taking place, the photographs that each person takes in their mind are seen as a joint creation. It is as if the couple were engaged at all times in a dance in which mutual recognition and the digestion/representation of the ongoing emotional experience are at stake.

As in the case of photography, sophisticated equipment makes possible new and refined forms of expression, but ultimately the key element is the photographer's eye, the sensitivity, the person, the history. You can take brilliant shots with ordinary cameras. In analysis, the moment of the shot, at least with the most felicitous ones, or of the choice (not for nothing do we say "chosen fact" or "selected fact") happens in the same way for an impulse that is felt as such and which is not the result of a rational decision. It is not "spontaneity" if I have a theory or model with which I can clearly and consistently justify this conduct and explain what its meaning is for the purposes of treatment.

Of course, as with a musician, talent can express itself at its best not when one knows nothing about musical theory and performance technique, but when these have been internalized to the point of becoming one with the person. Conscious and unconscious factors contribute; they cannot be separated. The *quiddity* that makes the difference remains an enigma; basically, it is about talent. And yet, for an artist, talent accounts only for a small percentage of skill. Everything else is work, study, experience. At least that is my experience. The vision that some have of the inspired artist or of the analyst-magician who disregards theories and models is a false vision – and I would go so far as to say unethical because it evades responsibility.

It is true, however, that there are also those who fetishize theory or technique and prove unable to exercise the "negative capability" that Keats saw as being at the origin of true artistic creation and that Bion borrowed in his theoretical discourse. In analysis, negative capability is the ability to carry out a kind of phenomenological reduction, to suspend everything that is already known. You put everything you know in the background and you feel as if you were watching an object, a scene you had never seen before. It is a simple but effective recommendation and, paradoxically, "impossible" to follow. When you cannot set it aside, as Freud urged analysts to do by using free association and fluctuating attention – a way of forgetting the logical meaning of speech in order to enhance the play of the body of words – then everything becomes flat and sterile.

If I had to pick an analogy with art, I would turn to a musical comparison. Exactly the same tune can be pure poetry if played by Coltrane, but most of the time, if performed by another musician, it is just technique. We could take other examples, Turner's marine landscapes or Bacon's disfigured portraits, and so on. So, what distinguishes ordinary photography from that which we consider beautiful enough to be worthy of being exhibited in a museum? Can we say that artistic photography manages to transcend the alienation of non-artistic photography? Does the special relationship that photography has with presence and reality make it an art form distinct from all others? Thinking of the metaphor of photography as an art that, like analysis, has a special relationship with the aura of the present, I recalled some books I had read in the past, notably Walter Benjamin (1935) and Susan Sontag (1977), and I think these could provide us with some further ideas on our topic.

For instance, Sontag criticizes photography when it is used as a means of *not* seeing but rather of taking possession of the thing – a criticism that could be applied to the style of certain cold, intellectual and mechanical analysts. Photographs or/interpretations then become an act of violence, of symbolic seizing of the other, of capture of the object. Insofar as it replaces the experience of reality, it becomes an alienating or anesthetizing filter with respect to what is seen and that often has to do with horror. At the Uffizi no one looks at the wonderful *Adoration of the Magi* by Leonardo, which has recently been restored. All are too busy documenting "I exist",

"I was there". Painting, Sontag writes, has never had such imperial ambitions. On the contrary, what seems important with photos is hoarding them, even though later one no longer looks at them. It is simply a matter of storage and accumulation.

This is an important aspect that unites analysis and photography, a certain relationship with the *immediacy* of experience, with the here and now, and which distinguishes it from other forms of art, for example from painting. Photography seems to guarantee immediate access to reality. Barthes is perhaps the writer who has had the most interesting things to say about this point. The essential aspect, as he emphasizes, is the presence of the photographer in the scene photographed. Analysis and photography have a similar relationship with immediacy, one might say with the Referent. By their very nature they have to deal with things that are present in the flesh. For photography, this means a special relationship with Time and Death. Since the person taking the picture cannot be absent from the scene, what photography always says is: "This was and I was there and I saw it with my own eyes". All art has to do with transience. Like analysis, it is a work of mourning, a way of letting things pass by giving them meaning, but for photography this relationship becomes special. The person photographed becomes a spectre.

But even in analysis, if its essence is the work of symbolization, it is always a matter of dealing, so to speak, with the *spectrality* of the object (the no-breast or the no-thing) or rather with the concrete absence held as a virtual presence in the name, and with the concrete presence lost as an absence in the name. As Žižek writes:

> as soon as the reality is symbolized, caught in a symbolic network, the thing itself is more present in a word, in its concept, than its immediate physical reality. More precisely, we cannot return to the immediate reality: even if we turn from the word to the thing – from the word 'table' to the table in its physical reality, for example – the appearance of the table itself is already marked with a certain lack – to know what a table really is, what it means, we must have recourse to the word which implies an absence of the thing.
>
> (1989, p. 131)

Perhaps we might then understand what is common to analysis and photography, a certain death drive, if by death drive we mean a life-giving drive – a "passion" for absence. The same absence that, if tolerated, is the source of life: for what, then, if not for beauty? Is this not what Freud means in his splendid essay "On Transience"? That beauty stands in a certain relationship with the ephemeral nature of all things? But, if so, then art has much to teach psychoanalysis and psychoanalysis also has much to say about art, as both set aesthetic experience as their ideal goal: that's where we restore body to the mind or mind to the body and we feel alive. For psychoanalysis, the aesthetic experience does not refer primarily to anything *aestheticizing*, but only to the dimension of meaning that we perceive as emotions.

Bion writes that even a psychoanalytic article must arouse emotions. And he wonders: "How many articles in the International Journal of Psychoanalysis have you read that were already dead?" And Winnicott: "Oh, God, may I be alive when I die" (Winnicott, 1989, p. 4). In an excellent essay from about twenty years ago, Ogden (1995) writes that any form of psychic suffering results from a limitation of the individual's ability to feel fully alive as a human being. What these immediate associations say is that the task of psychoanalysis is much broader than solving psychic conflict, eliminating symptoms, expanding the ability to reflect on oneself and take the initiative, but it has to do with promoting the experience of feeling vital and with the fact that the aspect of vitality should be considered an analysis "in its own terms" (Ogden, 1995, p. 19), hence the modern emphasis on creativity and play. So, what does it mean today when we talk of cure in psychoanalysis? If we think of the writings of the analysts we like best, we all find this characteristic of being vital. There are texts that breathe and texts that oppress. In the former, the language is everyday language, the analyst expresses a genuine interest in getting to know the patient, acknowledges his or her own emotions and uses theory with delicacy. In the latter the analyst usually puts up walls of theory and jargon, often takes on a moralistic tone, like a talking cricket, and frequently appears cold and insensitive.

The invisible girl

And yet, if I have chosen to approach our subject starting from the concept of vitality, it is because the main idea was given to me by an analysis session with one of my patients, whom I will call Anna. Anna tells me that one day she realized everything was always fine in her life, so good that nobody noticed her. Instead, she often feels empty inside. She is brilliant at her studies, but her emotional bonds are poor, not long-lasting, scarcely nourishing, lived without great enthusiasm, rather dull.

At a certain point she also fails in the area where she has always been admired, and falls into depression. There is intense family pressure to get back on track as soon as possible. However, despite having recovered from slipping into depression, Anna feels that she must put on hold her usual life as a perfect girl, and she shifts her interests in a "neutral" field. She is fully involved in a sporting activity. It is completely secondary with respect to her professional objectives and proves to be a decisive test for her attempt to restructure emotional ties within the family. This new life, removed from the practical and utilitarian purpose of study, work and success, becomes the gym where she tries to regain vitality in her main relationships. There Anna is worthy because she is herself and not because of the exams she passes with flying colours. Her parents' attention is not directed at practical purposes and she can really feel recognized and safe.

To illustrate this point, namely how important it is to feel that one is loved for oneself and not for what one can do, I would like to introduce a vignette from another patient, taken from a supervision session. I will return to the theme of vitality later on and to the question of how in analysis it should not be left to the humanity and spontaneity of the analyst alone, but ought to become a theoretical and technical parameter as well.

Halloween

This is the text of a supervision. At the beginning of a session, a patient, J., recounts: *"A strange dream: We were at R's house, it was a courtesy visit. A man in his 30s. . . . He's heavily made-up and wears an earring. He says: 'Surprise! It's me! and he turns his cheek* [but instead of "cheek", the text says "check"] *so that I can kiss him, but I am reluctant to kiss him and I just embrace him."* In the dream, dangerous animals and other very threatening characters arrive.

If seen as a real transformation in hallucinosis – that is, as a fragment of a dream dreamed in the waking state that expresses the attempt to give shape to an unconscious emotional experience – the slip of the pen by the colleague who presents the case is a felicitous event in the process of building the sense and meaning of the session. We have a surprising reformulation of the aesthetic conflict according to Meltzer (1986) fixed in the classic image of the child who agonizingly questions the sincerity of the mother. "Check or cheek?", here the patient is asked – and asks the object. The consonance of the two words evokes in me associations with Halloween and with the fateful question that children ask when they knock on their neighbour's door: "trick or treat?" J. suspects that he is dealing with a witch and not with a mother. This transformation gives us the opportunity to understand the unconscious emotional atmosphere that pervades the relationship at any given moment, and whether it is vital or not, to try to re-establish harmony with the patient.

This vignette also helps us realize that the dream of the analytic session continues in the act of writing the account and then in the shared dream of the supervision session. The association with Halloween is mine, and moreover in this case I am not even the analyst, but from the point of view of the theory of the analytic field one can rightly say that the association does not come from me but from *us*. This theory postulates that there are always unconscious exchanges between minds that generate an emotional field and unconscious field fantasies, whose meaning is more than the sum of the elements that make it up if taken in isolation. On the other hand, in order to give oneself an "I", a body must be animated by the presence of others. For psychoanalysis, the mind is the one *among* individuals. The *I* is *us*, its fabric is woven by the infinite threads that connect us to each other, in essence therefore the "I" is a web of relationships. To expand the "I", therefore, it is necessary to connect more "threads". The capacity that human beings have acquired through biological evolution is to know how to stretch these threads among themselves. To cure in analysis is to weave threads of humanity, to expand the psychic container. The threads are the phantasmatic projections of each one into the other and the emotions that accompany them. It is on these threads that the definition of authentication (authenticity) as "making legally valid" is based.

It is not true, as some say, that the container/contained dichotomy is a false problem, because between the two there is a very precise hierarchy. In today's psychoanalysis, the content of truth that nourishes the mind is such only if it respects the capacity of the psychic container to accept it. Bion (Bion, 1962) uses a curious image to describe the relationship between container and contained. Imagine the container as if it were a sort of grid of fabric sleeves connected together, and the fabric made of many intertwined threads of emotions. There is more. As a three-dimensional medium in which content is suspended, it then indicates "tolerance of doubt" (p. 94). When the relationship between container and contained is "convivial" (in a more technical sense, between preconception and realization; for example, between the innate expectation of the breast and the experience of breastfeeding), both grow. Bion ends up even talking about "convivial abstraction" (*commensal abstraction*) to say how a proto-concept of body order is formed, a kind of habit or sensitive idea or procedural scheme: nothing more than a component of what philosopher Merleau-Ponty (1945) calls body-intentionality.

Let's go back to our two vignettes. If we read Anna's dilemma in light of the second clinical fragment, it's easier to guess what her problem is. She is facing not only an enigmatic object, which is the rule, but an object with respect to which mistrust *prevails* over trust. Anna expects the witch and the poisoned apple and this becomes the lens through which she looks at any bond. The question is: okay, it is already important that a person has the ability to get in touch with the feeling that he/she has of him/herself and to express this sense of emptiness, but what does it mean to feel vital, and especially *how can one give vitality back to someone in the cure?*

First of all, it must be said that this awareness is not always there. The person may feel absolutely vital while in fact lying to themselves. And the meaning of vitality is elusive. The word is not found in Laplanche and Pontalis's *The Language of Psychoanalysis* (1967). The Treccani Dictionary[1] of the Italian language tells us that it is the *aptitude to live*. We cannot identify it with a set of ideational contents, although they may be part of it. Nor is it just the tone of how it is assessed in psychiatry. It is more something of the order of feeling that one has of oneself at any given time. But can one give oneself a sense of vitality? I would say no. The most difficult thing to understand, or the least immediate, is that, apart from the components of temperament and the contingent aspects of life, the sense of vitality is a social fact. *I can only feel vital in someone's eyes.* In these eyes you must be able to reflect yourself in a way that makes you feel content, in essence loved. You *become* yourself through this mirroring. If you feel coldly reflected, something inside you remains silent, inert, sterile, indefinite. Sometimes this happens. There are people who function in a de-personalized way in their life, that is, on the basis of a split between mind and body, because they have been recognized in their intellectual talents but without real warmth and affection. That is why, when other solutions have not worked, the only way to be seen may, as in the case of Anna, be failure.

The elements most directly connected to the feeling of vitality are emotional; they are embodied memories, procedural schemes, fantasies in the body (Gaddini, 1982) and therefore cannot be expressed in words and concepts except indirectly. That is also why we nowadays put so much stress on the role of the analyst's person; certainly not to fall into a kind of uncritical sentimentalism in which each is a measure unto oneself without any comparison with the others. This is something that is impossible, since one cannot remove oneself from the field of sociality expressed in language. One can lose oneself in non-consensuality, which is a very different thing. Let's do a simple experiment. Let's imagine having to refer a loved one to a therapist. Would we not send him or her to a person we know is expert and capable professionally but also empathic and vital? If it were a surgeon, it would not be the same. Why? Because for analysts these personal parameters also bear a theoretical and technical significance.

U-turn->you-turn->turn->turn-you-up

A. tells me a nightmare in which *she leaves her house at night and every time she wants to make a U-turn but can't. At some point, she arrives at a military post where they tell her that, given her work, she could stop there because the next day they are expecting a delegation from the psychiatric hospital.* The reason seems to be the climate of alarm (the "militarization") that there is in the family because of the imminent loss of an elder member who is severely ill. They are all anxious about the situation. But this narrative, which is reflected in the dream, can also be understood as an allegory that speaks to the moments of separation of various kinds in the analysis instead.

With a pun, the point is that U-turn as withdrawal from relationship is heard and transformed first into *your-turn* or *you-turn*, or even *turn-you-up*. Who? An external and internal object, or the analyst, so that he can realize the situation, becomes receptive again and placates A.'s anguish. In this case it is the transformation from *U-turn* to *you-turn* that organizes a field of meaning, opens new perspectives and indeed becomes a function of containment.

The essential factor in this transformation is the *surprise* effect that accompanies the transition from confusion and anxiety to something that seems meaningful when viewed in the light of context. Without this emotional element it would be something purely conceptual, cold and mechanical. Narrative transformations in the analytic field are not *merely* narrative because the selected fact that on each occasion organizes them "is the name of an emotional experience, the emotional experience of a sense of discovery of coherence" (Bion, 1962, p. 73). At the heart of this precious moment lies the possibility of accepting and understanding the other, of instilling vitality.

You see the meaning of working in the here and now. The analyst uses a phenomenological criterion: obviously the analyst takes into account the past of the patient and always reacts with humanity to the patient's pain and the history of the suffered traumas, but the analyst also "brackets them off" to focus on the level at which the intervention might be more useful to the patient. There is a kind of *epoché*. The analyst looks at things as if having never seen them before: *de-realizing* or *de-concretizing* them. The reality that the analyst is concerned with is the one on which the analyst can act most directly – the psychic reality. Actually, meaning is created through the construction of an intimate climate in the therapeutic relationship. It is as if every time the analyst had rediscovered that he or she is not a silent witness but a central character in the play that each time is staged in the theatre of analysis. If the unconscious does not lie behind or under, but within the conscious and vice versa, and therefore *always* speaks, and not only when it escapes the control of the double censorship hypothesized by Freud, even the stories of real traumas and concrete situations of the patient's life must necessarily always mean something else. Moreover, being attentive to the unconscious plane of communication does not in any way prevent us from acknowledging what the patient has suffered or is suffering, but adds another significant layer of meaning. On the other hand, apodictically sticking to the value of history as a sort of rocky layer of the psyche, removed from any possibility of unconscious signification, is both naive and in certain cases even irresponsible.

Nowadays the analytic couple is seen as continually engaged in a process of mutual recognition or, in other words, of subjectivation; as in a process of constant negotiation of the reciprocal status as *person*. This is specific to the field of analysis. In short, the role of emotion is strongly asserted here as an *(en)gram* or *pictogram* with respect to essential facts such as the process of self-construction of the subject, and the feeling of vitality. This also reflects the clinical experience that tells us that what patients suffer from is that they cannot contain (transform) emotions that are too violent. *The unknown of O* (unconscious proto-emotional experience of the relationship) is then the emotional position occupied by the patient and the analyst on the map that charts the vicissitudes of the relationship. In analysis only this really deserves to be investigated and everything must be directed towards the goal of the emotional encounter.

This is why for Bion only what is under the eyes of analyst and patient can be known:

> In psycho-analysis any O not *common* to analyst and analysand alike, and not available therefore for transformation by both, may be ignored as irrelevant to psycho-analysis. Any O not common to both is incapable of psycho-analytic investigation; *any appearance to the contrary depends on a failure to understand the nature of psycho-analytic interpretation.*
>
> (Bion, 1965, pp. 48–49, my emphasis)

But this precept is the most widely disregarded in clinical practice, often also by analysts who base themselves on Bion's theories. The impulse to cling to the concreteness of reality, historical or present, is simply too strong. This is the kind of attitude that Ferro (2017) ironically styled "*Bion à la carte*", because it avoids making the effort to confront Ferro's radical reformism, as expressed, for example, in the following paragraph:

> Psychoanalytic "observation" is concerned neither with what has happened nor with what is going to happen, but with what is happening. Furthermore, it is not concerned with sense impressions or objects of sense. . . . Every session attended by the psychoanalyst *must* have no history and no future. . . . What is "known" about the patient is of no further consequence: it is either false or irrelevant. . . . The only point of importance in any session is the unknown. Nothing *must* be allowed to distract from intuiting that. . . . *Obey the following rules.* . . . *Do not* remember past sessions . . . *no* crisis should be allowed to breach this rule. . . . The psychoanalyst can start by avoiding any desires for the approaching end of the session (or week, or term). Desires for results, 'cure' or even understanding *must not* be allowed to proliferate. . . . These *rules must be obeyed* all the time and not simply during the session. . . . If this *discipline* is followed, there will be an increase

of anxiety in the psychoanalyst at first, but it *must not* interfere with preservation of the rules. The procedure *should* be started at once and not be abandoned on any pretext whatever.

(Bion, 1992, pp. 380–382, my emphasis)

Bion also explains why it is so difficult to adhere to these principles:

a) Increased anguish because there is no barrier against fear of recognized dangers.
b) No barrier to guilt because there is no known substitute for the recognised and conventional therapeutic purposes.
c) Isolation from group key assumptions (*ibid.*, p. 296).

If the most effective way of helping patients acquire affective competence is through the filter of the current relationship with the analyst, then the truth of what happens cannot be solely cognitive. Nor is it enough to use *any* emotional reaction, for example as a counter-transferential response, if still read in a unidirectional sense. In addition, one must engage deeply in the relationship and therefore feel the burden of responsibility for what is happening in it. If it is not something that has *already* happened or that happens *elsewhere*, but that happens *here and now*, one can try immediately to improve the atmosphere of the encounter. Letting O "evolve" or "become" means not taking refuge in hasty and abstract interpretations of the facts of the analysis but encouraging the development of emotional-experiential knowledge. From this perspective, Bion's entire work can be seen as a radical attempt to reposition psychoanalysis (theory and practice) in the area of the unconscious, dream and body – not the anatomical body but the lived body.

Another obvious meaning of this theoretical and practical approach is that the *direct* and *continuous* emotional involvement of the analyst that takes place each time, moving along the lines of a centripetal strain, brings the discourse back to the dream of the session, and therefore to the therapeutic relationship, and makes hyper-amplified signals available to the analyst to map their respective positions in the analytic field. If, for example, a patient recounts a childhood memory or an event from current life, the analyst can only have indirect knowledge of it and try to empathize with the patient, perhaps by using a conscious identification. If instead the analyst reads the same memory as an unconscious communication related to the living emotions of the present relationship, the analyst will have some kind of direct cognition – a lived cognition, to be precise, one that is less inclined towards K and more towards O. And not only that: like any unconscious transformation, the perspective he takes from it will be richer and more "real" than any other that is confined to conscious experience. It is not that the analyst cannot know anything about the patient if the analyst values the historical or reality content of the patient's speech; rather, for the purposes of the analysis, and on the basis of all the premises listed so far, the second way of knowing carried out through referring everything to the here and now is more relevant. In other words, just like the scalpel of the surgeon, the main instrument of the analyst is a radical notion of receptivity with respect to the unconscious functioning of the minds in the here and now of the session. Receptivity to the productions of the unconscious allows the analytic couple to generate meaning and thus to expand the space of the dream and of inner life.

Note

1 www.treccani.it/vocabolario/vitalita/

References

Benjamin, W. (1935). *The Work of Art in the Age of Mechanical Reproduction.* London: Penguin, 1994.

Bion, W.R. (1962). *Learning from Experience.* London: Tavistock.

Bion, W.R. (1965). *Transformations: Change from Learning to Growth.* London: Heinemann.

Bion, W.R. (1992). *Cogitations.* London: Karnac.

Civitarese, G. (2014). *Truth and the Unconscious.* London: Routledge, 2016.

Civitarese, G. (2018). Vitality as a theoretical and technical parameter in psychoanalysis. *Romanian Journal of Psychoanalysis*, 11:121–138.

Ferro, A. (2017). *The New Analyst's Guide to the Galaxy: Questions about Contemporary Psychoanalysis.* London: Karnac.

Gaddini, E. (1982). Early defensive fantasies and the psychoanalytical process. *International Journal of Psycho-Analysis*, 63:379–388.

Laplanche, J., & Pontalis, J-B. (1967). *The Language of Psychoanalysis.* London: Karnac, 1988.

Meltzer, D. (1986). *Studies in Extended Metapsychology: Clinical Applications of Bion's Ideas.* London: Karnac.

Merleau-Ponty, M. (1945). *Phenomenology of Perception.* London: Routledge, 2002.

Ogden, T.H. (1997 [1995]). Analysing forms of aliveness and deadness of the transference-countertransference. *International Journal of Psychoanalysis*, 76:695–709.

Premoli, P. (1913). *Vocabolario nomenclatore*. Milano: Sonzogno.

Sontag, S. (1977). *On Photography*. New York: Farrar, Straus and Giroux.

Winnicott, D.W. (1989). A reflection. In: D.W. Winnicott (Ed.), *Psychoanalytic Explorations* (pp. 1–18). Cambridge, MA: Harvard University Press.

Žižek, S. (1989). *The Sublime Object of Ideology*. New York: Verso, 2009.

Chapter III

Attacks on linking, or uncontainability of beta elements?

In the brief commentary which prefaces the Italian edition of *Attacks on Linking*, S. Bordi (1970) calls this work one of the greatest contributions to the expansion of M. Klein's thought, and emphasizes how it is thanks to this paper that the concept of envy of the breast finds a place in the dialectic of the instincts.

Furthermore, in Bordi's opinion, Bion's paper gives the same weight to the features acquired during development as it does to those linked to the internal world and the instincts. In addition, it distinguishes those internal objects that belong to the Ego from those that are delegated to the Superego. I would now like to make a close and systematic examination of the work's theoretical aspects.

An interesting early observation concerns the assertion made by Bion at the IPA Congress of 1957 that the analogy between psychoanalytic and archaeological research had meaning only if addressed to the examination "not so much of a primitive civilization, as of a primitive catastrophe", and indeed his claim that the catastrophe we are seeking shifts in the very moment at which we study it is evidence of his divergence from Freud, who thought in terms of a leisurely examination, and also from Winnicott (1974) who in his famous "Fear of breakdown" wrote of a breakdown that has already happened.

Bion goes further and establishes *ante litteram* the concept of the "analytic field", in whose presentness all the events of the analysis occur. Indeed, it gives us pause for thought that, without theorizing it, Bion frequently uses the term "analytic field" in this work, and this is no cooled deposit of lava, but fluid, flaming lava, constantly appearing just below the surface of the field. The phenomena of eruption and evacuation are occurring in the very moment of our search. One of the destructions caused by

DOI: 10.4324/9781003279020-3

this proto-emotional magma, full of consequences, is that of the curiosity whose absence will prevent learning.

Another very useful way in which Bion clarifies matters is that he puts us on guard against considering a part-object as if it had an anatomical structure "because the part-object relationship is not with the anatomical structures only but with function, not with anatomy but with physiology, not with the breast but with feeding, poisoning, loving, hating". It would be difficult not to see in these observations, expressed in terms of alpha function, the germ of a concept which will be catastrophic for all preceding models of the mind.

In the face of the catastrophe, we cannot ask ourselves "Why did it happen?" but only "In what does it consist?"

It is at this point that Bion gives a wonderful description of what, when better organized, will become his model of the mind and will shift the interest of analysis away from contents to "tools for thinking dreaming feeling" (Ferro, 2010). He treats projective identification as a normal mode of functioning, one that is able to create a link between analyst and patient or infant and breast. There are analyses in which projective identification becomes the principal mode of communication, whether because the patient has not sufficiently developed from this modality, or because the analytic situation itself gives the opportunity for this modality to develop. Here Bion has a stroke of genius which will open up his strongly relational theoretical model, the "better connected patient" and "without memory and desire": the patient sometimes "felt there was some object that denied him the use of projective identification".

And who is this object?

It is the analyst himself, whose mind may not be sufficiently receptive of such projective identifications, or – though receptive – may have been overwhelmed by receiving them, as can often be the case in the primary relationship between infant and mother.

The patient who is prey to fears of annihilation tries to project them into the analyst, in the hope that they can remain in the analyst long enough to be renewed and transformed, but this hope fails if the analyst tries to be free of them too soon, bringing about an increase in distress and in the projective identifications themselves, which will become ever more violent and undermining of the analyst's mental functioning.

In a sense, what we see here is a description in different words of the model of the mind subsequently postulated by Bion: a mind will be able to develop if there is the capacity to evacuate (project) beta elements (sensorialities) into another mind that will be able to accept them, allow them to stay, and transform them by means of its own containing-transforming capacity into alpha elements (pictograms). These will be restored to the evacuating mind, but together with the method (or the functioning of the method) of alpha function, so they themselves can perform such functions as containment and transformation.

It is a brief enough passage from alpha elements to their concatenation in waking dream-thought, and on into the ability to dream (by day and night). In other words, the sensorialities dealt with by the analyst's capacity for Reverie will give life to the development of the mental that coincides with the oneiric, with the ability to dream. Situations of negative Reverie which prevent this process can occur if there is a surplus of $\male$ contents relative to the $\female$ capacity. In these cases – which can be caused by a sort of mental vaginismus in the other, or by an occlusion through excessive anxiety already present in the other's mind (and also simply in a mind too encumbered by theory), or by an excess of projected beta elements – we will have a dysfunction of the whole process which Reverie should have brought to the development of the mind (including the capacity for living the emotions), so an inversion of the alpha function will occur, and there will be evacuative phenomena of transformation in hallucinosis.

But let's go back to Bion in 1957 (the year when this paper was presented). He finds himself still straddling two theorizations: one that looks at the object (whether analyst or mother) and its possible dysfunctions, and another that looks at the patient (or infant) as the bearer of a primary "aggression", which is, however, insufficiently amenable to melioration by the receptive mind of the other (and it cannot be otherwise because the very experience of acceptance may give rise to envy or hatred). The first of these theorizations seems to allow more room for the capacity of a mother-analyst who can accept "nameless dread", or the fear of dying which dwells in the patient and the newborn infant.

Primary destructiveness? – or secondary destructiveness following the failure of the earliest relationships?

We are very familiar with this unsolved question, which I am tempted to answer in this way: we happen to be a species with a surplus of beta elements and ♂ in relation to alpha function and ♀, as a result of which there persist clusters of beta elements that erupt like uncontainable and untransformable tsunamis which are not destructive in themselves but have inescapably destructive effects on the landscape against which they strike.

Incidentally, in these particular pages we see how a new model or a new theory can come to life, in a sort of titanic struggle between mourning, the capacity to accept transience, and creativity that still causes a degree of catastrophic change in the theories which had briefly reconciled us, as Grotstein reminds us in his *Do I Dare to Disturb the Universe?* (Grotstein, 1983).

Returning to Bion and his courage in saying that the link between patient and analyst, or between infant and breast, consists in the mechanism of projective identification, I would like to give my chapter the title "Attack on the capacities for projective identification". The source of these attacks can be either partner in the analytic or mother-infant couple.

Bion suddenly seems frightened by the inspired direction he has taken, and looks for a compromise which may give him some necessary peace of mind in asserting that innate elements have the greatest importance as far as relationships are concerned; despite the importance of acquired elements, primary aggression and congenital envy remain the pillars.

At this point Bion speaks of "attacks on the analyst's peace of mind", and I see in this emphatic statement, beside the emerging concept of the patient's destruction of the envied good mental functioning of the analyst, the disturbance that the theoretical change of focus and his own genius are causing him in opening up new and (in relation to previous theories) unorthodox thoughts.

Well-functioning projective identification enables us to study our own sensations through the effect that they produce in the person who receives them. If this is made impossible, either because the mother is unable to function as a "storehouse" or because hatred and envy prevent the mother from carrying out such a function, then the link between the infant and the breast is destroyed and, as emphasized earlier, the capacity for curiosity is compromised.

If there is an obstruction on the path that would allow the infant to face up to violent emotions, this creates the preconditions for the total elimination of vitality. Every type of emotion brings hatred upon itself until all emotional life vanishes. If the development of emotional literacy fails in the proto-emotional states, the way is opened for de-affective functioning, Asperger's or autism, with hatred for any form of emotional life, and hatred of life *tout court*.

The centrality of the projective identifications and their vicissitudes becomes ever clearer, not only for mental development but also for mental functioning and, as I have already pointed out, for the ability to dream, feel and think.

If projective identification fails in its functioning, one of the consequences will be that the external object seems hostile to curiosity and to the "method" with which the newborn tries to satisfy it; and this will establish a severe Superego, incapable of truth, and an exaltation of moral demands leading to the formation of -($♀♂$), which sterilizes everything and denies every emotion and all development.

To conclude this part I would like to say that even if we allow the concept of "an innate destructiveness" (one that is not merely the consequence of a relational failure, however early) I think that at the heart of the matter we would still have the technical problem of how to transform this (supposed) "O" by means of a dream or, rather, by a journey through column 2 of the Grid – that of lying but also of dreams (Grotstein, 2007, 2009) – and of how such an "O" could be transformed by the metabolizing digestive activity of that "psychoanalytic field" where it finds itself at work, as a mass of beta elements in search of a dreaming and narrative function.

I would like to play a game in this second part: to see how I might view Bion's clinical material if it were brought to us today. I say "game" both in the sense that it only concerns fragments of material used as examples by Bion himself, and so we in fact know hardly anything about them; and in the sense that I enter into it fully aware of being a "dwarf" on the shoulders of a giant, a giant composed of Bion and the theories that he would develop subsequently. This game of mine aims to be an admiring homage and an acknowledgement of how Bion would develop from 1957 onwards. That will be the viewpoint from which I shall play, practicing on his "supposed clinical material", at least as I have understood it. (Or rather, as I have invented it, but I find this useful in showing the generative power of Bion's thought, his theoretical and conceptual monument, which is still waiting to be "absorbed".)

So let me play, bearing in mind that the game can also help us see Bion's model at work.

a) Bion intervenes to emphasize to the patient the positive feelings he is expressing towards his mother, who had been able to welcome an *insensitive baby* like him.

This interpretation, judging by the patient's response is, to say the least, premature and guilt-inducing (he calls the patient insensitive, and congratulates himself on his own availability to the patient).

The patient, the field's touchstone, responds as if he had received a mouthful too large to swallow, makes movements as if he were having difficulty swallowing, emits gurgling sounds like someone under water, and feels overwhelmed by the interpretation, submerged in it, flooded by it.

I recall that Bion himself (1989) in his *Clinical Seminars* will say that an interpretation may be given six days, six months or six years after having been thought, and that an interpretation must match the patient's ability to take it in, otherwise it would be like launching into complex explanations of the functioning of the digestive tract with a baby.

> b) The patient complains that he can't sleep any more.
> Bion suggests that if he slept he might dream.
> The patient replies that he feels "wet" and weak.

Bion thinks that feeling wet, soaked, is to do with urine and with the attacks that the patient would have made with his urine through envy and hatred. Looking at the sequence of verbal exchanges, I would have thought of a patient on the alert because he does not know what distressing interpretation may be coming his way, and who in his fear is squaring up for a fight.

Here too some passages come to mind from the *Clinical Seminars* in which Bion urges us not to give excessively saturated and exhaustive interpretations, and suggests instead that we ask ourselves "Which story is one to tell?" One story that could be told, in my opinion, is that of an infant who is too alarmed to sleep and who, not understanding what his mother is saying to him, drenches himself in pee out of fear.

c) We do not know how the session starts. Bion considers it reasonable to interpret the patient as being present at a sexual encounter between two people. The patient "reacted as if he had received a violent blow", and Bion gathers that the blow was his interpretation. When the patient seems to have been stabbed with a knife, Bion interprets that he is having hallucinations (of "seeing an invisible object"). Rather than recognizing his own interpretation as a knife-blow, Bion disavows his intervention.

We are light-years away from what Bion will say in his *Italian Seminars* (1985): that the patient is capable of describing precisely the analyst's mode of being and operating.

d) After some isolated remarks ("which had no meaning for me") the patient says he feels understood by a girl he has met, and then shudders.

Bion tries to draw the patient's attention to these shudders.

The patient, in his role as satellite navigation system, replies that the room has been filled with a blue haze: in other words, it seems to me, Bion's attempts had been felt as "polluting".

Here too we are in the presence of an analyst who knows too much, who decodes everything instantly. There is not yet the fruit of those "negative capabilities" of which he will speak years later, nor of that extension into the field of myth, passion and meaning (Bion, 1963) which he talks about in *Elements of Psychoanalysis*.

e) Bion notes that the patient makes "statements of fact" and adds that Bion would not understand them.

Bion, returning to the contents of the session from the previous day, interprets that the patient feels bad. The patient's response is that he felt there were "two probability clouds" in the room. This would make me think of two possible ways in which the session could develop, or of a weather-forecaster confused about the way the weather/session might turn out.

Here too we are a long way from the Bion for whom the unsaturated, negative capability, and work towards the "selected fact" will be key points in his way of working.

f) After half an hour of silence the patient announces that a piece of metal has fallen onto the floor. I shall pass over Bion's interpretation about envy, saying that perhaps I would have thought the patient means, "it seems to me that a silence like lead or iron has fallen between us".

I merely note that Bion seems in these clinical examples to be looking for a confirmation of the theory he has in mind. Naturally he is playing a psychoanalytic game (which will later become that inspired psychoanalytic game which is the Grid), putting together a patchwork of different patients and sessions; I have embellished this with my own game, the point of which is to show that Bion's theorizing was ahead of its application in the consulting room.

I think, moreover, that all the brilliant later development of his thought and the theorizing yet to come are an immense legacy for psychoanalytic theory and technique that we are a long way from having understood and utilized.

In "Attacks on Linking" we see a genius at work in the moment of a catastrophic change from theories that are his own and that give him peace of mind, to theories under development that torment him, besides catastrophic changes that allow him new thoughts and new technical formulations.

In saying this, I have in mind *Learning from Experience*, *Elements of Psychoanalysis*, and *Transformations*, but even more that wonderful treatise on psychoanalytic technique and theory dramatized as *Memoir of the Future*.

We see in the Bion of 1957 a genius not yet recognized as such, who is making "anticipatory hypotheses" and who dares – while at times retreating into the familiar – to open up the Unknown, the world beyond the Pillars of Hercules, and who will be a Christopher Columbus revealing new and terrible conceptual universes.

I would now like to move towards a conclusion, and in this third part play another game, which I will call "a dwarf on the shoulders of a giant", in which I will share some developments of Bion's thought that have occurred to me during an acquaintance of over thirty years with the Bionian oeuvre.

A child in analysis draws for us: Stefano

I would like to describe some drawings made by a child in analysis, which it seems to me enable us to visualize both the process of his mental growth and to configure a model of the mind that I think is the one we can derive from Bion.

At the first session Stefano starts by telling a story: there were some skeletons who were walking around in the desert . . . they were an army of skeletons . . . these skeletons had been shot out of caves.

I think of Stefano's black rage, how he is turning himself into a robot, his pathological evacuations, his battles with skeletons. But how can I not also think of the mass evacuation of beta elements? How can I not think of primitive projective identifications in search of reverie functions?

Some months later he draws a house in a tree with a separate bathroom. At the base of the tree there is a tunnel. At the bottom of the tree there are bombs that might explode (like proto-emotional states). Inside the tree there is a bomb which has been defused by a bomb-disposal expert. I think of a humanization, an animation, of an emerging mental functioning, and of the appearance of hollow spaces apart from the newly created "bath-ing" function. What is appearing is a mind capable of reverie and able to accept projective identifications, which thereby find a place and become thinkable.

The months pass and then he draws another picture during a session. Between two trees there is a house suspended on ropes, and reachable by the ropes. The occupants are making soup. Are they expecting guests? A helicopter is transporting a cargo of fruit. In the meantime, they are hav-ing a party. How could we not think of a relationality coming to life? We see the arrival of characters and multiple roles, of sociality, of exchange. An emotional field has come to life; the projective identifications now alphabetized allow the formation of waking dream-thought, and a narra-tive coming into being.

In reworking the previous picture, Stefano adds some very deep roots underneath, which contain plentiful provisions. In addition, there is a cav-ern with a disco beneath it and a "reflecting lamp with mirrors" as in real discotheques. Underneath there are rooms for smokers and non-smokers, and other rooms awaiting designation.

How could we not think of the long journey from mechanization, from beta elements to the constituting of a mental function (alpha), and then the beginning of an ever-stronger relationality which puts down roots with affective contents, and thereby develops tools and constructs spaces for fantasy to work in and for generating the Unconscious?

Of course, I do not know how this may look from other standpoints, but from my point of view as an analyst who has observed, and observes, what goes on in the consulting room, the presence of the mind of the Other is indispensable for the birth of the psychic. Naturally the Big Bang of the birth of the psychic Other will be followed by the long journey to sub-jectivize "O", which will become the tolerable "O" for that specific mind and be digested, depending on the enzymes and coenzymes of which that mind, or rather that field, has been able to make use.

The hieroglyphic mother and the Rosetta Stone

Carla is a girl aged 7 who, on starting school, was found to have a general delay in acquiring language, and difficulty in reading and in memorizing the vowels and some consonants.

She has a younger sister who suffers from moments of intense fear.

Their mother is described as warm and affectionate, alternating with moments of emotional incontinence. From the start there emerges the idea of a child who has had difficulty reading her mother's state of mind, which is now welcoming and receptive and now frankly convex, rebarbative, rejecting. The mother too seems unable to find her way among Carla's states of mind, describing her as a puzzling child.

Carla's affective foundation seems disorienting in its alternation of unpredictable emotional states UU∩U∩∩∩CCU which have not allowed her a safe standpoint from which to take in these differences: how is Mamma at this moment? What can I expect from her? And also, the symmetrical question: what are my feelings towards Mamma? Do I hate her or can I not do without her? The "foundation stone" and its shape are fundamental for the development of the capacity to distinguish another person's emotions (or mental states) and indeed one's own.

The indecipherable mother is an impossible hieroglyph to read in her alternation between concave and convex, partly concave, partly convex.

The situation Carla is exposed to is like driving home and turning into the garage, but never knowing whether the garage door is open or merely a "*trompe-l'oeil*" against which the car will crash.

We could represent all this with the hypothetical sequence UU∩C∩∩CU∩ or its underlying effective level ♀♀♂♀♂♂♀♀♂.

This narrative of serious difficulties in reading the mind of the other comes up again in a double story begun with great distress by the mother: at school, the teacher told her, Carla seems not to distinguish or recognize even those classmates with whom she has a reasonably good relationship. She goes up to them calling them "Friend" indiscriminately.

There is no clear recognition of Filippo, Luigi, Marcello, just as there is none of the vowels or other letters that she cannot distinguish, and she does not remember whether her tummy sticks out at the front like a b or at the back like a d.

Her father confirms this "reading", recalling their honeymoon in Australia and meeting a variety of people in the house of friends, where nobody was ever formally introduced. Everyone called each other "Mate", creating a certain lack of differentiation.

I should also add the fear felt by a part of her (her younger sister), finding all situations indecipherable.

In the consulting room is she with a "friend" or a Bluebeard?

What does her grandfather mean when he says "I'll give you a party?"[1]

It is also true that her parents, while lacking in discriminatory function and the ability to identify states of mind, have been sufficiently able to transform the swarms of sensoriality so that Carla had no need for the compulsive focus on details which occurs in the paranoid scenario.

The situation I have described is enacted immediately in the session, where Carla does not know whether she wants to hug or strangle the therapist, and he himself is unable to decipher what the girl is about to do. It is true that the session will become progressively the place of discrimination where Carla and her therapist will learn to understand, accept and differentiate the components of the fundamental emotional grammar that is being developed as the affective text of the session.

Suddenly Carla goes through a brief period of near-madness in which she fears that people (and emotions) are wearing masks, and that characters are appearing out of a television serial about armed robbers called "the wolf", "the pig" and so on, but Carla tries to evade these by masking her toys.

At the same time she starts games in which she puts fierce animals (which she is now able to distinguish from tame ones) inside toy saucepans, as if she felt the need to cook them; or as Bion would say, she lives the need to tame wild thoughts.

The field evolves

The analytic field is also the site of all the patient's and analyst's potential identities, which does not mean that all the potential identities must come to life or be integrated: sometimes is it appropriate for them to remain split off or buried within the strata of the field itself for the whole of the time in which this will be useful for the development of mental life.

For a narrative to develop, as Diderot remembered apropos *Jacques the Fatalist*, there are so many possible stories that must be "put to sleep" so that the main story, the "daughter" of the two co-narrators, can come to life and develop.

I have spoken elsewhere of how there are two "loci" of mental creativity in a Bionian metapsychology: the place where beta elements, carriers of all the sensoriality, are transformed via alpha function into pictograms (the sub-units of dream-thought in the waking state) and the place where the derived narrative in all its infinite variety, on a longer or shorter leash, moves away from or stays close to waking dream-thought within the field (Ferro, 2002, 2009; Ferro & Civitarese, 2015).

In Simenon's fine novel *Les Clients d'Avrenos*, the protagonist Nouchi tells how when she was a child on her way home from school, she would often observe from behind a fence her sister, only a few years older, giving herself to adult men in exchange for a few coins or chocolate. It was the poor Vienna of the early twentieth century. Then Nouchi becomes an *entraîneuse*, a hostess in a low-life bar, though she remains "frigid".

I have purposely chosen the telling of a neutral episode so as to see the various models at work.

In a model based on historic reconstruction it is not hard to anticipate where it would take us: to the childhood traumatic experience, child sexuality, abuse and then the acquaintance with pain.

A model centred on Nouchi's internal world could take us towards eroticized destructiveness and an attack on linking.

An intermediate field model could lead us to a reading like this: an infantile part remains as an observer of what happens in the field; that is, the analyst is coupling with a more adult part of the patient, who gains warmth and sweetness from this but remains nevertheless "cold" because the interpretative coupling has been premature. But I would like to take Ferro further (1992à2014) in order to open up a field understood in a totally different way. That is to say, we don't know it at all: we must merely postulate a field in development, but in doing so surrender all its predictability, or at least accept that what we are given to know is Fo (Field-0) while we wait for F1 . . . 2 . . . n.

We cannot therefore postulate that the field will be decipherable except in the moment t(0) at which it occurs, but this moment also gives birth to infinite other possible fields that will come to life and be selected by the movement of the potential multitude that is the "couple", and will be knowable only *après-coup* with the opening/closing of infinite possible fields, derivatives of infinite factors, many of which are unknown.

For a long time, too long a time, we thought interpretation was the engine of analysis, an oscillation between time and abstinence/presence and intervention.

The initial episode of which I spoke could in fact produce any number of possible stories.

This could be the starting point of an exercise using a range of writings with different outcomes.

Or equally, different directors could develop different films based on the same outline, the same plot.

(Even if it is not clear what the role of "director" might be in the session or from what it might be constituted.)

From among all the hypotheticals I would prioritize the "atmospheric" factors of the session and the links formed by multiple and variable reveries with multiple and variable projective identifications.

There is more creativity in not hindering developments than there is in specifically initiating them.

The "chiacco"

In Sicilian dialect the term "chiacco" indicates a kind of noose made of rope suspended from wires, usually between opposite or adjacent balconies, for hanging out washing to dry. If something light, a sock or handkerchief, is hung from this it shows the strength of the wind. A patient in analysis tells me that his grandfather used to watch something hanging out to dry so he could see how windy the day was: though the wind was usually a gentle breeze and not the Bora, the north-eastern gale which sometimes batters Palermo.

From the "forecast" given by the movement of something hanging from the "chiacco" the grandfather would determine the day's risk of catching a cold or cough from the "change of air" – that is, the wind if he was outside, or the dreaded draught if he was indoors.

This could be seen as an anecdote about childhood and as the source of eventual hypochondriac anxieties. Or it could be seen as a warning present in the internal world; or if seen in moment "0" of the field, as the description of an alarm-signal for some emotional current possibly about to come to life.

The description of a field in which possible differences in potential, in temperature, in heat could be dangerous because they would activate currents difficult to control.

In that case the emotions would be winds that could cause illness.

But if we move from time 0 towards time 1 . . . and on to "n", we have no way of foreseeing what type of field will develop or what narratives will give meaning to the emotional lines of force that will have come to life. One exercise could be, having set this field to time 0, to describe its possible developments.

In fencing, and even in the very different kind dependent on marking thrusts with electrified jackets and weapons, there is still a basic set of terms: parries, circular parries, hits, feints, double feints, arrests, a "counter", "two counters" and so on, but it is the sum total of these that makes every fencing match – for the knowledgeable spectator – a unique, unrepeatable and above all completely unpredictable experience, because it is the fruit of a combination of variables tending to infinity.

All this could also apply to the development of psychoanalysis, where every change could be experienced as a turbulence to be avoided, even though we cannot evolve without disturbing what we know.

Note

1 Translator's note. Carla knows that her grandfather's innocent phrase is also gangster slang: "I'll wipe you out", "I'll waste you".

References

Bion, W.R. (1963). *Elements of Psycho-Analysis*. London: Heinemann.

Bion, W.R. (1985). *The Italian Seminars*. London: Routledge.

Bion, W.R. (1989). *Clinical Seminars and Other Works*. London: Karnac, 1994.

Bordi, S. (1970). In: W.R. Bion (Ed.), *Analisi degli schizofrenici e metodo psico-analitico* (p. 143). Roma: Armando, 1967.

Ferro, A. (2002). Some implications of Bion's thought: The waking dream and narrative derivatives. *International Journal of Psychoanalysis*, 83:597–607.

Ferro, A. (2009). Transformations in dreaming and characters in the psychoanalytic field. *International Journal of Psychoanalysis*, 90:209–230.

Ferro, A. (2010). Navette per l'Inconscio: rêveries, trasformazioni in sogno, sogni. *Rivista di Psicoanalisi*, 56:615–634.

Ferro, A., & Civitarese, G. (2015). *The Analytic Field and its Transformations*. London: Karnac.

Grotstein, J.S. (Ed.). (1983). *Do I Dare Disturb the Universe? A Memorial to W.R. Bion*. London: Karnac.

Grotstein, J.S. (2007). *A Beam of Intense Darkness: Wilfred Bion's Legacy to Psychoanalysis*. London: Karnac.

Grotstein, J.S. (2009). Dreaming as a 'curtain of illusion': Revisiting the 'royal road' with Bion as our guide. *International Journal of Psychoanalysis*, 90:733–752.

Winnicott, D.W. (1974). Fear of breakdown. *International Review of Psycho-Analysis*, 1:103–107.

Chapter IV

On Bion's concept of container/contained

The concept of container/contained (♂♀) has its origin in Freud's concept of projection, in other words, the unconscious fantasy of ridding oneself of those aspects of the self that are unacceptable to the ego and attributing them to someone else. In Freud, projection is above all the anatomical phenomenon whereby nerve bundles start from the surface of the body and travel to the brain. There are more fibres that enter than leave each area of the brain and at the central level one single delegate represents several voters. This then becomes the model for psychic projection and condensation, which is one of the mechanisms of dream rhetoric.

With Melanie Klein, projection becomes projective identification. In keeping with her view of an internal world populated by crowds of actors, partial objects that work together to weave the threads of unconscious life – the glasses through which we read or, it would be better to say, construct reality – it becomes possible for the subject to do away with a disagreeable content and identify it with a content or object in the other. Projective identification is also thought of as a process that occurs between internal objects within the same individual. What is also described is the concept of projective counter-identification – here too, first seen as a pathological event and later as the ability to tune in to what is received.

With Bion, projective identification stops being just a pathological defence mechanism and becomes a physiological mechanism that is part of human communication. In an article on this topic written in the late 1970s, Ogden (1979) places even more emphasis on the effective interpersonal pressure that is brought to bear so as to compel reception of what is projected. Projective identification now becomes fully relational or intersubjective. From the perspective of the analytic field, we can say that the

DOI: 10.4324/9781003279020-4

unconscious field of the pair is generated by the interplay of projective identifications (Ferro & Civitarese, 2015).

There remains a certain ambiguity between the idea of being colonized by the other and receiving communications; but this ambiguity is also inherent in the definition of subject as an entity constitutively alienated by the Other. Furthermore, given the knowledge we now have of mirror neurons, we can imagine much more vividly how this "mysterious" transmission can take place. There is no longer a clear distinction between perception and action. Understanding the other, what he or she is intimately feeling, is also based on inherited mechanisms of the embodied simulation of action. This may explain why we are sometimes moved by scenes in second-rate films that we don't even particularly like.

If the concept of (♂♀) is the successor to the concepts of projection and projective identification, it has however also been influenced by Winnicott's concept of "holding". The concept of (♂♀) is more abstract than Winnicott's notion and implies a higher level of generalization. It is as if we had proceeded not from images of all the trees in existence to images of trees of different species but to the very concept of the tree. Bion's intention is to subsume under the same concept *several* concepts coming from different psychoanalytic models so as to heighten psychoanalysis's level of formalization or scientificity. In this way he hopes to put an end to the so-called Babel of languages and the religious wars that are waged among psychoanalytic institutions.

The formula is brilliant in its simplicity and closeness to the experience of practical life. Examples of concrete (♂♀) relationships are: mouth/nipple, vagina/penis, group/individual, mother/baby, etc. The important thing in each case is the nature and quality of the connection that links the two terms of a (♂♀) relationship. Container/contained relationships are always multiple and reciprocal – and virtually infinite if we also take the lowest levels of interaction into consideration. The baby holds in its mouth the nipple, which contains milk, but in the meantime, it is also held by the mother's arms; and both find themselves in broader contexts that support and sustain them, and so on and so forth. As a tool, (♂♀) is extremely powerful and versatile; one might almost say "obvious". If it is the successor to the concept of projective identification, it is however reborn as a sexual metaphor – as is also reflected in the male and female symbols Bion chose to represent it – or as a metaphor of the mind as a digestive system.

What must the mind digest?

The mind is constantly engaged in "digesting" the primitive or raw sense data that arise at the interface between soma and reality, and in transforming them into cognitive maps, urges to exist and value systems. It must constantly gather and process information adaptively for the purpose of survival. Once processed, proto-emotions and proto-sensations become, as it were, clothed in thought. They become thought along a continuum that runs from the procedural and the bodily to the opposite extreme of the concept, or maximum abstraction. It is fascinating to observe how this apparatus for psychic transformation works. It is something that usually escapes our notice. While we are exposed to some external or internal stimulus, an image arrives and surprises us, and it can be an association or a reverie. It offers us a possible solution in the form of a metaphor, an allegory, a micro-dream, a poem or a musical form.

To take an example: I am attempting to explain to a patient what it means to be loved for oneself and not for one's concrete achievements – we are trying to understand why he finds speaking during analysis such an effort – and in a flash two childhood friends of mine come to mind. One has made little or nothing of his life, while the other has become a big name in his professional field. The emotional bond I feel with both of them has nonetheless remained equally intense. Here the path to understanding took me through the sorrow I felt at my first friend's partial failure in life (at least according to conventional standards) and the emotional work it cost me to process my feelings.

Another example. I have an important oral exam coming up; I am anxious even though I am not fully aware that that is how I feel and the night before the exam I dream that the examiners are centenarians with sagging skin and wrinkles who speak to me in a language I don't know. The meaning is clear: be on your guard!

A third example: in a supervision session a highly capable woman analyst describes how a normally boring and evasive patient of hers criticized her harshly. She got very upset and reacted angrily, attempting to engage in a rational discussion about what the therapy had, or had not, achieved. What had happened here? The colleague had taken up a defensive stance, as she was unable at that moment to contain her anger, or to find other meanings for it – the idea, for example, that for that particular patient "arguing" might have signified coming out of her autistic shell.

In the discussion we had – and having created a situation in which another mind was available to dream what the colleague had been incapable of dreaming – we came up with some metaphors and sayings that helped us understand other possible aspects of the violent emotions that had assailed her. Some examples: the idea that projective identification enabled her to say that she realized how the patient felt (at least, more or less) about her love objects; the view that people have of love as a quarrel; or how important it is when bringing up a child to get it to play-wrestle or to let it win at draughts, and so on.

One last example: I arrive at a neuroscience conference. I know nobody there. The other speakers all project slides with anatomical images of the brain. I wonder what I'm doing in this place, a quack among "real" scientists. I expect them to be sceptical. Then suddenly "I see myself" in the classroom where I attended neurology lessons at university. So the place is not entirely foreign to me, I think. At that point my anxiety subsides. It is as if I had digested the unfamiliar and transformed it into the familiar.

Bion (1970) speaks of the concept of ($\male\female$) at great length in Chapter VII of *Attention and Interpretation*. He describes the ($\male\female$) relationship as that which obtains between the mystic or genius or messiah and the institution. The mystic allows the group or individual to experience the "truth" directly; he is the one who claims to be in unison with the deity, God, in the sense of O or the real. Obviously, Bion (1974, pp. 73–82) makes no concessions to mysticism, yet he does adopt some fragments of its discourse, figures and terms, for his own purposes, so as to exploit its "penumbra of associations". The group needs "a continued 'supply of genius'". Similarly, it can be said that the individual "should be ready to produce a 'flash of genius'"; also the individual "can be regarded as constantly attempting to achieve union with the deity". Also important to note is the difference between group and institution:

> The function of the group is to produce a genius; the function of the Establishment is to take up and absorb the consequences, so that the group is not destroyed . . . the institutionalizing memory [is intended to] 'contain' the mystic revelation and its creative and destructive force.

The mystic and the group are figures that stand for the contained and the container, respectively. The mystic may destroy the group if his or her truth cannot be contained, or the group that has turned into an institution may stifle at birth the mystic/messianic idea if it feels too threatened. However, there can also be other interactions that involve mutual growth. Significantly, Bion adds that the "configuration that represents the relationship between the mystic and the institution can be recognized in, and be the representation of, the relationship between the emotional experience and the representative formulation (words, music, painting, etc.) designed to contain it" (*ibid.*, p. 85). In these words, we catch a glimpse of the transition from the "evidential" to the "aesthetic" paradigm in psychoanalysis.

The (♂♀) relationship describes an interaction between two elements with different characteristics that can bring about transformations. After all, the concept reflects the essential dialectic of subjectivation. It is impossible to do without either the work group or the institution, because both are essential to the development of the individual. Clearly, such a situation finds a precise correspondence in the relationship between a given mental condition of the analysand and psychoanalytic interpretation. It is essential to bear in mind the other's real ability to accept the new, otherwise even something that is true for the analyst may prove to be traumatic.

The Rain is a Danish TV series about a deadly virus spread by rainfall. It depicts an apocalypse. A family manages to take refuge in a secret safe shelter. The father has to leave the shelter in order to save the others, so he instructs his elder daughter about what to do. He tells her the truth but explains that they can't tell her younger brother anything because emotionally he wouldn't be able to cope with the situation.

If the container hardens and no longer accepts something new, it becomes devitalized. At this point, as Bion puts it in his idiosyncratic language, the "rabbinical directorate" (*ibid.*, p. 75) gains the upper hand over the mystic – the one who claims to have, or has, a direct relationship with the "deity", with the truth. Obviously, resistance to the new is something within each of us. It should not be thought of only as a force of external resistance. For this reason, the analyst should not "desire" to cure, and in order to "see" he should "blind himself". Memory, desire and understanding obstruct sight of the new and stand in the way of intuition of the unexpected.

The fact is, though, there are not enough "mystics" and we cannot expect all mental health professionals to be able to stand such strain. The world's work, Bion writes, has to be done by ordinary people. Another way of saying this is that there is inevitably a lot of routine in psychotherapeutic work and that we should not demand too much of ourselves. If we did, the risk is that this stance would turn into a form of narcissistic closure.

The concept of (♂♀) is also useful in explaining the controversies that exist between the different schools of psychoanalysis. Bion writes:

> I have not always felt 'separated' from someone who differs from me in the theories he holds; that does not seem to me to afford a standard of measurement by which the gap can be measured. Conversely, I have felt very far separated from some who, apparently, hold the same theories. Therefore, if the 'gap' is to be 'measured', it will have to be in some domain other than theory. The differences in theory are symptoms of differences in vertex and not a measure of the differences.
>
> (*ibid.*, p. 86)

What does this mean? It means that any group (even an "internal group") can turn into an institution, and a rigid institution at that; it also means that the real difference lies between those who manage to maintain an emotional state of receptiveness to the new and those who close themselves up within their certainties. What matters most is whether the perspective one adopts is authentically designed to unearth diversity and emotional truth or – regardless of which theory, Freudian, Kleinian or Bionian – whether it is instead conceived to saturate the search for the facts of the analysis with the "already known".

Not being able to transform/contain emotions leads to all kinds of suffering both for the individual (within his or her internal group) and for the group. To illustrate this thesis, I will now turn to two films: *Locke*, by Steven Knight (2013), and *Ida*, by Paweł Pawlikowski (2013). Then, with the aid of a short clinical vignette I shall attempt to show how the emotional work of containment/understanding in analysis requires that the therapist should know how to use his or her own subjectivity to the full.

Locke (d)

The film features no action scenes, chases or spectacular crashes. Yet the narration has the pace and feel of a truly exciting thriller. The main action of the film has Locke – a Welshman, as his broad accent reveals – driving along a motorway in a BMW SUV. The protagonist of Steven Knight's eponymous film (2013), with Tom Hardy as its sole actor, is on his way to a London hospital where a woman he met on a "one-night stand" is about to give birth to the child they conceived together. A journey of ninety minutes. However, at the same time his wife and children are waiting for him to come home to watch a football match. What is more, he is a construction engineer who the following day is due to face the most demanding task of his career. It will be up to him to ensure that a huge concrete pouring operation for the construction of a fifty-five-storey skyscraper is carried out correctly. Nuclear plants aside, it will be the largest ever construction project in Europe. More than two hundred trucks will be converging on the same area at the same time, requiring complex coordination. Huge amounts of money are at stake. But Locke will not be there, because, even at the cost of losing everything, he has decided that he must put his life in order: work, children, wife, himself. Not what anybody would expect from someone like him. Locke has always been a person known for his great self-control; he is mature, measured, reliable, precise, tolerant, methodical.

What we witness therefore is a tough contest in which a middle-aged, middle-class, successful but not exceptional man, who clearly serves as a mirror for the spectator, allows himself for once in his life to lose his head. What we understand, however, is that he is losing his head in order to find it. The viewer immediately senses that the whole film will take place inside the cramped space of the car (a man-machine? a man locked up in a place of psychic refuge?) and for a moment we feel the same sense of claustrophobia that Locke himself is experiencing. One thinks of *Gravity* (Alfonso Cuarón, 2013) or *Buried* (Rodrigo Cortés, 2010), two films in which the central metaphor is that of a relationship with an object that is either too claustrophobic or too agoraphobic. In this sense, the title already suggests a possible interpretation. From the beginning to the end, the protagonist of *Locke* is seen as in effect "locked" inside the shell of his SUV. But, more importantly, this state serves as an allegory for other levels of being where he has closed himself off: at work, in his marriage, in his extra-marital life. All the containers that should lend vitality to his existence have hardened; they now spurn the new and fill him with a sense of suffocation. Locke tries to save himself and to do so he embarks on a sort of journey – literally – to the end of (his) night.

The film could be a dream or, rather, a nightmare told to an analyst. It even unfolds like an analytic session. The setting is carefully marked off. Only one character is physically visible, and he is the only one who speaks on camera. It is also night-time, which makes one think of dreams and the beam of darkness that Freud thought the analyst should cast on things to illuminate them. The spectator is witness to a constant game of mirrors between several characters. All the shots showing Locke's face reflected in the car door window and rear-view mirror allude to this game. What's more, overlaid red and yellow lights from street lamps and headlights glide over Locke's face and become the lights of his thoughts and emotions.

No other characters are seen, but they can be heard on speaker phone, suggesting their quality as inner, disembodied voices. Like a chess champion playing multiple games simultaneously, Locke grapples with his life in a series of frantic calls: with his boss, entered in his list of contacts as the "bastard"; with Bethan, the woman he got pregnant; with his son waiting for him at home; with his other son who has left him a message on the answering machine; with Katrina, his wife of fifteen years; with the policeman who has to regulate the traffic to get the lorries to the site on time; and lastly with Donald, his semi-alcoholic and panicked assistant, to whom he has explain what to do when standing in for him the following day. But the most powerful presence that is felt is that of the ghost of his father. A father never really buried. Locke addresses this conscious and unconscious internal presence in a fury, as if it were some imaginary passenger in the back seat, with the rear-view mirror performing the function of memory. Here again, it is almost as if he were expressing an intense negative transference to an analyst sitting behind him on the couch.

For Freud, the transference relationship is a battlefield where neurosis can be vanquished. It cannot be done "in effigy". This is why change involves taking risks. If he wants to achieve change, Locke must deal with the trauma that has left its mark on him. He must go on a journey that enables him to relive virtually the relationship with his irresponsible father, Laius, who abandoned him at birth. Here then, at least in the first part of the film, Locke is the father who himself is in danger of abandoning a son. He doesn't know and we don't know if he will make it. Taking responsibility for one's internal world and the characters who inhabit it is only possible by going through a painful experience. Just as Locke tries to control a very difficult situation from a distance, so too, despite being very close, we sometimes perceive the emotions we have to master as distant and difficult to manage because they cannot be grasped and manipulated like concrete objects – neither with the hands nor with the senses.

The challenge of constructing the skyscraper thus immediately takes on the meaning of a powerful metaphor that accompanies the protagonist throughout his journey. There is no better embodiment of the enormous emotional difficulty Locke is facing all of a sudden. After all, he needs inner calm to withstand the anguish and anger of his various interlocutors – the many virtual presences that throng his mind. To contain their anguish is to contain his own. Outbursts of anger are thus interspersed with more peaceful moments. In the end, Locke succeeds, perhaps because another important character in the film is the GPS navigation system. We could think of it as an alpha function that enables him, albeit at times with difficulty, to keep the transformative processes of his mind active. The director has himself stated in an interview that *Locke* is a film about "containment". We might add, about the containment made possible by the object's ability to engage in reverie.

The extraordinary thing is that almost half of the time the topic of conversation is cement – not exactly the stuff of movies! If this narrative moves us it is because what Locke is talking about applies to the skyscraper, to the film and to life. A solid foundation is also what is needed for life. Locke realizes that in order to live, and not just to survive, he must take care of his emotional ties, which are what make life worth living. To do this he must first of all exist himself, he must feel alive. He has to take responsibility for both his children and his inner world. Not only for his conscious feelings and conscious identifications, but also for the unconscious ones represented by the parental *imago*. At one point Locke realizes with horror that he is actually about to behave just like his father had done with him.

The film makes us reflect on how many people are so closed off within disastrous relationships with their parents that they cannot think of anything else all their lives. Like animals caught in a trap, they continue to struggle desperately to free themselves. They live in the past to such an extent that this generates a sense of disquieting wonder in the analyst, who apart from theoretical knowledge of them should in fact also be used to such situations. To use speculative language, we might say that a "closed" individual is like someone who has lost the openness that is the distinguishing mark of "being there", the quality that makes us different from animals, what in the Heideggerian concept of *Dasein* is expressed by the particle *da*.

Like any self-respecting hero's journey, this is also a journey of transformation. At the end of the film we realize that Locke has been able to loosen the grip of bonds that made him suffer. In Bion's language, not only the child manages to be born, but also the new (messianic, brilliant) idea that can so easily be suffocated or that might in its turn shatter the container. No more the repetition of the identical "It's always been" blazoned on the side of a lorry Locke passes by on his journey. In the end, Locke manages to become in all respects the father he did not have, both to his children and to himself. As he says regarding the fragile and unhappy woman who is about to give birth, he too has a right to be happy.

Id(e)a

Ida tells the story of a young novice nun who was abandoned as a child and has since been brought up by nuns in a convent. So, she was taken in by a "total" institution – a rigid container that can be seen as a metaphor for "non-concrete" and entirely mental containers that are entirely commensurate to the explosive force of the emotions that could drive her crazy were she to give them free rein. A week before she is due to take her vows, the abbess suggests she should visit her aunt, Wanda, so as to finally take leave of the world outside the convent walls. Perhaps this is a way of helping her to re-integrate painful aspects of herself she has pushed away and to make her decision a more conscious one. Through her encounter with Wanda, Ida discovers many things about herself and her family of origin. In striving to embrace this potentially destructive new content, she attempts to become more "human".

So, a black-and-white Polish film about a young nun who is about to take her vows? At this point, Italian viewers, accustomed as they are to the narrative grammar of Hollywood films and as presumably contented consumers of popular American television series, will probably be reminded of Paolo Villaggio as *The Second Tragic Fantozzi* struggling to watch Eisenstein's *Battleship Potemkin*. But this film is a completely different proposition. Once we have got over our initial reluctance, we become fascinated by the magic of great cinema.

As we watch this film, we rediscover the part that stunning cinematography can play in rendering the subtlest of emotional nuances. The film is complex and convincing partly because it effortlessly plays various levels off against each other: the historical level, the here-and-now level of the relationship between the characters, the level on which the characters are seen as internal presences within Ida and therefore as intrapsychic, and lastly the level that includes the viewer in his or her creative response to the film. It is clear that the viewer both films/watches the film and is filmed/watched by it.

For the purposes of our discussion about emotional work in analysis we can think of Ida as an "idea". What we hope to achieve with our patients and with ourselves is to have ideas about how to make sense of life that are both new and good, rational and "sensitive". Ida's life is the same as any new idea; she can die, live or close herself off in a *claustrum*.

The film is constructed around some obvious binary pairs, suggested first and foremost by the decision to shoot the film in black and white. The effect is to transport us to the early 1960s, but by deliberately choosing not to use colour the director also sets up the opposition between past and present more effectively than by the straightforward use of an historical setting. Further opposing pairs are: faith/atheism, morality/debauchery, victims/perpetrators, communism/post-communism, Catholics/Jews, openness/seclusion, spirit/body, Ida/Wanda, Idea/body, virgin/prostitute, drowned/saved, asceticism/depravity, faith/cynicism, Catholicism/Judaism, guilt/redemption, etc. The list gives an idea of how many different paths the interpretation of this film can legitimately follow.

What truths are these pairs meant to represent to us? Ida's journey is more an attempt to deconstruct than to reinforce these oppositions. There is a sanctity about baseness, as Dostoevsky teaches us, and a baseness about virtue. The past is in the present as the present is also in the past. The saved become perpetrators and vice versa, as we see every day in the many places on earth where disaster strikes. At this point we have already invoked one of the principles of Bion's method, namely that of caesura, seen not as a clear line of separation but as an area to be navigated through and an instrument or symbol of an inclination towards the systematic exercise of doubt that is both ethical and epistemological; an exercise whose purpose is to expand the area of what we can think (in other words, accommodate in the mind) and tolerate. For the sake of mental health, the point is not so much what is true in the absolute sense, but how much truth/thought is bearable (containable) for the individual and for the group.

The film "works" as a kind of psychoanalytic road movie or journey of discovery. It expands our mind and helps us take responsibility for ourselves, or rather the host of characters we are made up of. It has the look of a black-and-white film but actually it is a film about life's infinite shades of grey. Nothing is ever just black or white. All we have are various tones of grey. The emotional work carried out by Ida, and by the viewer who identifies with her, consists in an attempt to free herself/ourselves from the hyper-luminous logic of binary oppositions.

The film-container introduces us to various institutions that are in effect real characters: the convent, the party, the mind, the community, the family. Each of them is responsible for dealing with certain contents. Some of these contents are potential killers (i.e., destructive contents). At a certain point in her life, Ida finds herself unexpectedly offered the opportunity for a change that could be called catastrophic – not necessarily in the negative sense of the term. It matters little that it was the abbess (perhaps, a maternal *imago* or split-off internal object that offers itself to be integrated with other "maternal" aspects represented by the aunt) who suggested she meet her aunt (perhaps, an initial truth/contained that is awaiting metabolization).

The relationship that establishes itself between Ida and Wanda is by no means easy. The film confronts the viewer with the question whether Wanda will manage to become more human in contact with Ida. Will Ida manage to become more human in contact with Wanda? Inside her, will the mother-abbess manage to blend with the Mother-Wanda?

The fact is that together they embark on a journey to discover Ida's family origins. (The essential mystery is always that of birth and death.) Along this path they come across several "truths". Wanda's bloody past and her present miserable life, Ida's discovery that she is Jewish, the holocaust, the betrayal and killing of her parents – all these emerge.

On her journey, however, Ida also encounters music, Coltrane's jazz, sensuality, youth, dancing, sex. We see her gradually removing the various articles of clothing that make up her rigid uniform; she "sees herself seeing herself" (to adapt the title of a wonderful book by Valerio Magrelli), and is seen with new eyes.

However, the aunt cannot stand the pain and takes her own life. It is as if this new trauma had pushed Ida to rapidly retreat into her shell again, this time for good, totally disillusioned and abandoned. In the end the idea (the new Id(e)a she has entertained inside herself for a while) cannot live on. Nonetheless, it is true that Ida is now richer and certainly more human and that her choice is at any rate more mature. Of course, Wanda can be seen as that which Ida cannot accept about herself and her suicide as the "suicide" in the form of seclusion that Ida embarks on by choosing poverty, obedience, chastity and simplicity. Even though Ida does not really open herself up to life, she will not be subject to the same seclusion she would have experienced had she not met her aunt. The fact is, we have all met humane nuns but also bad nuns – in other words, nuns who are doubly cloistered.

In conclusion, it would seem that from a psychological point of view the integration of the Abbess-Wanda into Ida was only partially successful.

As a final point, I would like to say something about what makes the film so powerful. Various factors contribute to this effect, but one in particular is worthy of attention. *The true protagonist of the film is not even Ida but the beautiful and expressive face of Agata Trzebuchowska, the actress who plays her.* The director lays great emphasis on this key to understanding the film. The incredible beauty of Ida's face is the beauty the newborn child sees in the mother; it is what Ida had been unable to contemplate sufficiently. As the film progresses, Ida's face becomes an intense and sensual presence that conjures up an intolerable absence. Indeed, by taking her vows, by hiding this face, it is as if Ida were acting out the absence of the other. By no longer allowing anyone else to look at her or allowing herself to look at anyone else or to see herself reflected in their eyes, this decision comes ultimately to serve in some way to represent her and thus to contain the pain and the anger that has been injected into her.

For the viewer, the beauty of the film clearly equates with the maternal face/breast that contains all anguish. As with any work of art, it is the form, the aesthetic quality that works. *Ida* is a beautiful film; it is intense and stark, moving and austere, spectral and elegant, compact, perfect and sensual. Before such a classic work, one is reminded of Bresson's minimalism, but also of a certain rawness we find in Haneke, the gift Bergman showed for exploring faces, and some of the atmospheres Antonioni was a master at creating.

The representation of evil is not the solution to evil; perhaps it is only a partial solution, yet nevertheless it is potentially redemptive (Civitarese, 2012). The absent face of the mother, whose very absence becomes persecutory, is obviously also the ferocious face of history (red Wanda, Wanda the butcher) as well as the ferocity that we all know is always lurking inside each one of us. The film thus demonstrates how pointless any truth content is if it is not related to its acceptability and thus to the availability of a container able to accommodate it.

The wolf-woman

Sonia arrives fifteen minutes late. Up to this point in her analysis I have always thought of her as a slightly boring patient. My impression is that there are no emotions circulating anywhere, that everything is flat. She tells me that she has had a really bad weekend and what's more that she will soon be getting her period and that "it's a full moon". The full moon affects her a lot. She has marked all the full moon days on her calendar. Then she tells me about her husband. They alternate moments of anger and quarrelling with other moments when they get on well together and enjoy their intimacy. But he often gets drunk or "smokes joints". When she picks him up on this they again start shouting at each other and arguing. But then occasionally he is considerate, he buys her flowers, gives her perfumes, helps her around the house. Immediately afterwards Sonia realizes again that when she hugs him, basically she feels nothing. She never smiles and has no interest in looking after the house. Her husband sees that she is unhappy, commenting how she is always fiddling around with her cell phone. She turns the remark against him. It is impossible to know which of the two is more unhappy. Behind all this lies their disagreement about whether or not to have a child. Sonia is afraid that if a child arrives (the new/messianic idea?), he might leave her. But her husband is also afraid that once the baby is born, she will leave him.

As I listen to her, I think that this is a couple immobilized by the impossibility of making sense of what is happening to them. There is a great deal of anger in the air, but they are also very attracted to each other. They are caught in a bond that has sadomasochistic overtones. Each is dangerous to the other, and yet they are unable to split up. They would like to change, but they are terrified that something new might steer them towards destruction.

In the meantime, I realize to my surprise that my previous impression was not true, namely that very little emotion was involved. So, when the wolf-woman comes onto the scene, I start to take a new interest in Sonia. "When the moon is full" the frustrated and dissatisfied wife unexpectedly turns into a dangerous animal that "takes bites out of" the session by arriving late and who depicts (me) (as) a husband who only seems interested in chasing after her and whose only solution to the problem is more or less toxic addiction and immobility (boredom?). It occurs to me that I come from the only region in Italy where wolves and bears still roam the mountains, a region whose inhabitants (that is, myself included) are said to be somewhat on the wild side. Yet at the same time, it also occurs to me that I am well acquainted with that region and also with its famous sheepdogs that are unafraid of wolves.

The question then becomes: how to transform the wolf into a sheepdog or how to safeguard the fragile aspects of both the patient's psyche and the analysis from being destroyed by wolf-like emotions? The full moon, the association with the ferocity and aggression of the wolf and then with my native region (here, the analysis) helps me to steer back to the dream of the session what until then I had treated as real and external (the husband, etc.). This produces a new ability to contain Sonia's anger as an emotion that concerns *us*. The full moon then also symbolizes the analyst's receptivity, the ability to understand the language of the unconscious, and, just like that special ability, it is both fascinating and illuminating. By virtue of its very weakness, it also sheds light on things we would rather not see, things *we would not be able* to see if we projected onto them the dazzling light of a rationality devoid of any intuition.

At the next session Sonia is late again and shows up bearing a cup of coffee. She tells me about one of her young pupils whose mother forgot to pick up after school (again, I picture my "bored" detachment and her loneliness), and that together they waited for the mother, which was the reason she was late for the session. She then adds that she has a terrible headache. I connect the two and tell myself that perhaps what impedes thought is her fear of separation and the fact of not being in attunement. Sonia keeps on talking about her husband and his fits of anger. She mentions an episode in which she was so furious she smashed her mobile phone on the ground, a violent gesture that demonstrates the impossibility of thought and is a way of releasing tension by vomiting it out. As always, this was followed by a quarrel, tears and then reconciliation. Significantly, Sonia comments: *"On the other hand, if I didn't fight with him like that, I would lose myself and my life"*. This, I reflect, is where the need for the "coffee" of anger comes from – the need for something that stimulates and revives. In short, it is clear that anger is both a symptom of the malaise and the glue that holds the symptom together. After each crisis, for a while anger functions both as an insulation and as a companion or substitute for the other. To repeat, I now understand that anger has been covered over in the session by "boredom" or has coincided with it both for her and for me – after all, isn't boredom a form of minor depression, and depression an unconscious hatred felt towards the object? Boredom stands in the way of any potential growth. But now a new idea (this very idea/interpretation) has managed to overcome the emotional barrier of boredom *qua* symptom thanks to the capacity to dream the session that has also been brought back to life in part by the way the images Sonia offers resonate with something very personal to me.

In this vignette I have tried to depict the psychic processes of transformation whereby meaning is created in analysis. By this I mean real emotional "work", which for the analyst almost literally implies "suffering" the understanding first hand (I use this term in the same way that Bion talks about "suffering pain" or "suffering pleasure" – in other words, as synonymous with an experience that is inevitably negative, that is to say, linked to the work of mourning). Listening, when carried out the way Bion asks us to do it – namely without memory, desire and understanding – means that memory, desire and understanding must be "suffered" or, one might say, "become". It means letting ourselves be involved in some way by the other in the most intimate sphere of our affections.

Place or process?

I hope that this close reading of two extraordinary films, together with the accompanying vignette, will have shown how fertile and versatile Bion's concept of (♂♀) can be as it takes us on a path towards a finer-grained understanding of the emotional life of the individual and of groups, and, tangentially, also of the meaning of the aesthetic experience in art. The concept of (♂♀) is an extraordinarily effective model for describing how the growth, creativity, generativity and nourishment of the psyche occurs. As we said, these are processes. It is not that we have some sort of anatomical container in the brain that takes in anything. The truth is rather that if we think about how intercellular communication and synaptic communication occur, it is always a question of material contents that can – or cannot – be accommodated in certain sites. The expression container/contained, which, as we have said, is essentially an abstraction from the Kleinian concept of projective identification, is however not dynamic enough. It would be better to say "to contain or to be contained" (Bion, 1963, p. 7). For Ogden (2004, p. 1356):

> The 'container' [in Bion's theory of the container-contained] is not a thing but a process. It is the capacity for the unconscious psychological work of dreaming, operating in concert with the capacity for preconscious dream-like thinking (rêverie), and the capacity for more fully conscious secondary-process thinking.

What is the outcome of this emotional work?

It creates "psychic sugars" that have to be burned immediately or else stored, and amino acids that need to bind together to create "psychic tissues". A meaning is created for the experience that can be immediately utilized while at the same time the structures designed to make sense of things are reinforced. What needs to be contained is the surplus that would otherwise shatter the container. An acceptable definition of the activity of thinking could be something like: "The act of taking away from the emotions anything that exceeds the individual's capacity to use them". The success of the operation always depends on two terms; it always expresses a relationship. If the container becomes infinite or if it is too narrow, the operation fails. Both in the inter- and intra-psychic dimension, these operations take place not only at an intellectual level but also at a semiotic, implicit and procedural level. We are endowed with knowledge of the body, with sensorimotor patterns that have been assimilated through semiotic interaction with the object, which also go to form the lens through which we read the world. They themselves can be overflowing, and even here, at times, have positive results. As Proust walks on the uneven paving stones of a Paris courtyard, he staggers, in other words his body loses its balance (it fails to "understand" the slight unevenness in the ground), but what is awakened is the memory of his visit to Venice, where something similar happened, and . . . the dream is set in motion, meaning is generated, sense-based ideas burst forth.

To use Bion's terminology: the proto-emotional or proto-sensory elements to be transformed are the beta elements, whereas the alpha elements are the product of alphabetization. These go to make up the alpha screen, the membrane that enables us to differentiate between conscious and unconscious, etc. If each alpha element corresponds to a micro-experience of the passage from beta to alpha, we can clearly see that the alpha screen is the screen that is constructed in the wake of an infinite series of moments during which we had a positive (unison) experience with the object, moments in which the object helped us make sense of what was happening to us, consciously and unconsciously. Ultimately it is a screen made up of human meaning – or in other words language.

Bion develops other notions to clarify which qualities the object-container should ideally possess if it is to foster the process of containing emotions. I mention only two of them here: capacity for reverie and negative capability.

The capacity to engage in reverie is the capacity to absorb the child's anxieties as part of a loving attitude towards him or her. This is an important point because it avoids seeing understanding/containing as a purely intellectual event. Not only must understanding be somato-psychic, it must also emerge from a desire, from an investment. Grotstein (2007, p. 291) provides us with an outstanding description of this interaction. Coming after Bion and Winnicott, he presents it as the model of what happens in analysis:

> As the mother does for her infant, so the analyst absorbs the analysand's pain by partial or trial identification ("becoming") and allows it to become part of himself. In his reverie he then allows his own repertoire of conscious and unconscious personal experiences to be summoned, so that some of them may be symmetrical to or match up with the analysand's still unfathomable projections (β-elements, O). Eventually, the analyst sees a pattern in the material – that is, the pattern becomes the selected fact that allows the analyst to interpret it (create a permanent constant conjunction of the elements).

It is equally true that we must learn how to deal with this desire for the other and also with the other's desire, and also how to make use of our negative capability, that is, the ability to contain the chaos, anxiety and sense of guilt we feel at not understanding immediately, without falling prey to disorganization, and waiting for a new meaning to form. In other words, even when wishing to understand, we should resist the desire for hasty understanding, and rather train ourselves to eschew it altogether. Only in this way can we place ourselves in the ideal state whereby we put our unconscious system of understanding or dreaming to work – in other words, suffering/"becoming" understanding.

Negative capability is connected to the emotional competence that is acquired by tolerating doubt. It is related to knowing how to allow the gradual development of a container. The contents ($\male$) that are the expression of a dominant paranoid-schizoid state, a "cloud of uncertainty" of beta elements, must be allowed to disperse and to remain in this state for a certain period of time before some surprise comes along to organize them into something coherent. As we have said, this container is not an abstract entity. The ultra-fine histology of its tissues is made up of emotions transformed into thoughts. The ability to tolerate doubt,[1] uncertainty and paradox gives this essential connective the qualities of elasticity necessary to host elements of ♂, and thus to make knowledge possible (for Bion, K), or rather O → K: not purely rational knowledge, but that which arises from being able to learn from experience, ultimately, from the introjection of the interplay between projective identifications and maternal reverie, and from the ability, which emanates from it, to use emotions within a framework of sharing.

In closing, let us once again ask the question: what is meant by the word "contain"?

We have said that it means making sense of experience – full, poetic, somato-psychic sense, human sense (the sense of animals endowed with a language-producing mind) – and not just broadening the self-awareness that is an expression of thought at its most abstract. The better we are at containing, the better we are too at recognizing the signal, the need, the desire for the other and for ourselves. While it may seem simple, this is not the case because ultimately every symbol or every word – the instruments used to attain this recognition – bears the sign of the absence of the other and arouses the terror that is always provoked by this absence. In short, every minimal act of symbolization, from birth onwards – therefore also including the pre-categorical and preverbal, implies a head-spinning struggle that is fought out between identity and difference – in other words, a struggle that is both risky and pleasurable.

Note

1 See Bion (1962, p. 92):

> For the model for the growth of ♀ I shall borrow Elliott Jaques's concept of the reticulum. . . . ♀ develops by accretion to produce a series of sleeves that are conjoined. The result is a reticulum in which the gaps are the sleeves and the threads forming the meshes of the reticulum are the emotions. . . . The model for the growth of ♂ is a medium in which lie suspended the 'contents'. . . . The medium in a commensal relationship of ♂ and ♀ is tolerated doubt . . . developing ♂ can be visualized as being similar to the elements of the paranoid-schizoid position but without the sense of persecution.

References

Bion, W.R. (1962). *Learning from Experience*. London: Tavistock.
Bion, W.R. (1963). *Elements of Psycho-Analysis*. London: Heinemann.

Bion, W.R. (1974). *Il cambiamento catastrofico. La Griglia/Caesura/Seminari brasiliani/Intervista*. Torino: Loescher,1981.

Civitarese, G. (2012). L'argent di Robert Bresson e la redenzione dello stile. http://www.stateofmind.it/2012/07/largentdirobertbressonlaredenzionedellostile/.

Cortés, R. (Director) (2010). *Buried*. Spain.

Cuarón, A. (Director) (2013). *Gravity*. UK, USA.

Ferro, A., & Civitarese, G. (2015). *The Analytic Field and its Transformations*. London: Karnac.

Grotstein, J.S. (2007). *A Beam of Intense Darkness: Wilfred Bion's Legacy to Psychoanalysis*. London: Karnac.

Knight, S. (Director) (2013). *Locke*. UK, USA.

Ogden, T.H. (1979). On projective identification. *International Journal of Psychoanalysis*, 60:357–373.

Ogden, T.H. (2004). On holding and containing, being and dreaming. *International Journal of Psychoanalysis*, 85(6):1349–1364.

Pawlikowski, P. (Director) (2013). *Ida*. Poland, Denmark, France, UK.

Chapter V

Divergences

In this chapter I shall attempt to bring out some of the main fracture lines that divide our model of psychoanalysis from others.

Narrative container

We believe that the time has come to develop the idea of container away from a spatial entity and towards something that has the quality of narrative.

A container is to be seen not as something that "contains" emotions – in the same way as a fence keeps in horses, cows or bison (or aggregates of beta, *balpha* or alpha elements) – but as a narrative that provides space for "facts", characters, emotions and the links that bind them together. Hulk, Django Unchained, Jack the Ripper, Jane Eyre and Aunt Piera can all form stabilizing bonds between them.

The narration of these characters becomes a fluid, ever-moving container that allows for the development of emotions and thoughts that become welded together and as such stop being uncontainable.

Narration mixes together and balances out the various components that come alive, and become thinkable, within it.

We have all seen those classic films that tell the story of two escapees from a maximum security prison chained together at the ankles whose first desire is to sever the chain that prevents them from moving freely. Here the opposite process takes place: the chain, the link between the characters is what makes it possible to contain them even more. If Jack the Ripper were roaming dangerously around the city, one way to limit his destructiveness would be to tie him to the terrible Hulk. Most importantly, together they would create the kind of fluid narrative that would make containment possible and allow new characters to grow. Less linear and more complex

DOI: 10.4324/9781003279020-5

narratives weave a narrative web that by its nature is better able to perform the function of containing.

We would now like to look at our divergences from those strong theories which, after decades in the analytic profession, we feel in a position to dissent from. Our aim is not to criticize them; indeed, they have been of great importance in the development of psychoanalysis. However, we now see them as remote from and alien to our current way of thinking.

We have taken this idea of divergences from a film by Neil Burger (2014). Fittingly, its title is *Divergent*, and in it, survivors of a war have bonded together to establish a peaceful social order by assigning people to one of four factions: "Dauntless", "Abnegation", "Candour" and "Erudite". This uniformity has produced a society of utter peace and quiet.

But there was also a group of the "Divergents", dangerous people who needed to be eliminated. These people had multiple attributes and thought in ways that meant they did not fit into any of the other predetermined categories.

What follows is a description of where and in what way we "diverge".

A) Infant observation

Infant observation used to be of great importance in the study of developmental psychology, but in our view, it now seems harmful as a way of fostering analytic mental functioning. For one thing, because it makes for a strong mother/child code of interpretation and consequently emphasizes this code to the detriment of all others, or at any rate hypertrophies it. Secondly, because the mind of the patient is important in its interaction with the analyst's mind and it is this encounter that triggers specific co-narratives, reveries, pairs. Thirdly, it provokes a situation of excessive asymmetry: on the one hand, adults/parents and, on the other, the child, and this produces "fixed" concepts. Finally, it leads the future analyst to compile a repertoire of prescribed reveries that leave insufficient space for the free creativity of the analytic pair.

B) The creativity of the analytic pair

Many analyses, many analytic models are like trams: they run on previously laid down, predictable tracks. There may be "switches" along these prescribed and partly rigid tracks, but the direction is always predetermined. "Trolleybus analysis" is different; it is more flexible but still limited. Lastly, there are also "four-wheel-drive off-road" analyses. You never know from one day to the next where they will take you, and there is always the chance they might even send you off on difficult and completely unexpected paths.

C) Transference-countertransference axis

This formula now seems hackneyed and above all not true. It speaks to the history of psychoanalysis and to the many invaluable studies of "countertransference" (alongside transference). However, it is like continuing to study Latin on the arrogant assumption that it helps develop a sense of logic in a world that speaks English or Chinese. For example, the clear non-distinction between the identity of patient and analyst in conceptualizations such as that of the field makes this concept obsolete and misleading given that in the session we have before us complex multigroup structures, with all the narrative nodes and transformations they can produce. The concept of "lateral transference" also becomes completely obsolete since the field is itself a multi-dimensional and multi-temporal web of lateral transferences.

D) Criteria (when to terminate analysis, what constitutes analysability, how to interpret a dream, etc.)

We find puzzling the idea that it is possible to rely on predictable and predefined criteria to answer any of the previously mentioned questions. These decisions are the result of a creative and unrepeatable act. In my opinion, an analysis may end when the field gives notice of its ending in any one of an infinite number of possible ways.

E) Not taking autistic nuclei into consideration

Autistic nuclei are much more present than we say or know, even though Bleger – with the concept of agglutinated nucleus – and Ogden – with the contiguous-autistic position – have made them cornerstones of their theories. Autistic functioning manifests itself in intolerance to change. We should remember how the agglutinated core becomes stratified in the setting and how it can turn into a tsunami every time the setting is altered.

Recycling

For the last few months, patient F. has been evacuating words and stories that make absolutely no sense at all. Having tried in vain to deploy the whole possible repertoire of psychoanalytic techniques (not only interpretation), I have given up, hoping for better times. At this point the patient announces she is expecting a baby. Something is being born, I tell myself, even if I'm not sure what it is or why it is happening. I even find myself regularly falling asleep, something that only happens with her. Nonetheless, I am confident that, as Bion would say with regard to the analytic field in an atmosphere of negative capability, "it evolves". One day I am surprised when she tells me that she has had a dream in which, *while doing the recycling, she fed her sister a huge quantity of plastic bottles and other non-recyclable plastic.* The dream perfectly chimes in with my experience of not having received anything that might sustain the analysis. I am able to tell her that we can now talk about something that is not plastic and I suggest that there must be things she would like to talk to me about. "Yes, there are, but I feel ashamed!" is her reply. Then, little by little, both incredible persecutory anxieties and previously unimagined erotic fantasies begin to emerge. . . .

F) Violence

Violence comes out in various forms: out-and-out violence, uncontrollable emotions, premature ejaculation, enuresis. One could talk about the inadequacy or fragility of the container. One could then move on to include defences against these (uncontainable) hyper-contents, taking in obsessiveness and phobias and so on.

G) Attention Deficit Hyperactivity Disorder (ADHD)

One could speak of this disorder as a deconstruction of panic attacks into many micro-charges that might explode and produce an inability to concentrate.

H) The problem of the obvious and the known

We have espoused concepts (such as the Oedipus complex) that cover up our lack of knowledge. We think of them as "spots of light", but in fact they are "blind spots". We are terrified of the unknown and for this reason we resort to violence to ward off this terror.

I) Analysis as an antibiotic

Plague analysis and Luis M. Cabré's question: "Should a patient tell the truth in the session?". But does this really matter? Arguably patients tell us more when they play the game of lying. We inevitably think of Pirandello's indeterminacy and the fact that our interest is focused not so much on content as on developing tools for thinking. At the recent FEP/EFP conference in Stockholm, José Carlos Calich quoted Bion: "Interpretive knowledge without love is aggression".

J) The obvious and creative

Hyperbole

A child or an adult patient – does it matter? – says he once grabbed a kitten by the tail and threw it off a balcony. The stereotype is: cruelty to animals. Alternatively, at random: a description of how he had to get rid of his feline, scratchy, aggressive or seductive aspects; Bionian "hyperbole" serves to get rid of dangerous things but impoverishes the personality.

Germany

A patient recounts how she was stopped at the border because she was attempting to smuggle in a "little monkey", whereupon she was put in prison; primitive or "arboreal" elements are not allowed to enter Germany. But where is "Germany" and above all what does it stand for in the consulting room?

Flammable substances

A patient who is getting over a period of depression he has been "treating" by indulging in a series of compulsive extramarital affairs has a dream in which *he spreads a thick, creamy substance all over the carpet on the first floor of his home. As he is about to finish, he realizes that it is a highly flammable substance and that if he had set it alight, as he had planned to do, the whole first floor would have caught fire and the house would have collapsed.* Incidentally he has also developed an undefined inflammatory reaction in both legs. I do not interpret the dream explicitly but only make some comments which lead the patient to conclude that setting his house on fire was not a good idea and that he will have to find other less "costly" methods.

Some random reflections

One criticism levelled at field theory is that it is supposedly superficial. What is often not understood is the centrality to analytic field theory of the unconscious and its ongoing construction.

In field theory the expectation is that an unconscious configuration will emerge for both analyst and patient and will be interpreted in continuous *après coup*. There is a significant difference between this and the concept of enactment. The latter occurs in a two-person relationship and always implies a past → present → past circular movement. Therapeutic action also differs from the functioning of the field, as in the latter case time is dilated and the first stage of the movement ("making unconscious", producing unconscious) takes place largely in a completely unconscious manner.

Voltage

A highly regarded colleague recounts a case in which a woman patient complains of abuse and is intolerant of proximity. He continues to offer her transference interpretations, not realizing that the field has contracted the patient's illness and is giving evidence of excessive voltage. The lamp can only tolerate 200 volts, but an interpretive voltage of 250 volts is constantly being used. Most of the time it would be enough to simply reduce this voltage to 180 (or sometimes less). This would avoid giving the patient the feeling of being the victim of overvoltage. Tangential interventions that connect and describe what is happening in the field would be of great value.

Destructiveness

One of the most common tendencies in psychoanalysis ever since its inception and throughout its development is its use of the death instinct, the death drive, or also the idea of destructiveness, to explain behaviour otherwise not so easily or immediately understandable (I am always reminded of the term "whim" used to label the way a child behaves when we don't understand what he or she wants).

I don't think this is the only possible way to make sense of such behaviour. In my view, a more useful idea is that our species has to deal with a surplus of sensoriality, proto-emotions or beta elements, only some of which can be contained and transformed or, in other words, can enter into the circuit of containers and metabolizations. The share of beta elements that is not subject to these processes remains free to roam and can only be evacuated with destructive effects – and this is precisely the result of otherwise unmanageable surplus shares. Another softer and less radical way of managing them would be to colour them pink ("pinkification"), in other words, by transforming them into a rosy vision, denying their harshness and conflict, or else through evacuative explosiveness, whereby explosions of lava-like rage ease tensions in the "system".

We now see the defence mechanisms we used to regard as oscillating between modalities along the PS ↔D spectrum as extending into the universe with various degrees of the CAP (contiguous-autistic position), which in my view includes what in other terminology has been called the glischro-caric position or the agglutinated nucleus, and which leads to all possible degrees of "Aspergerization".

Child abuse

This concept can be seen from many different points of view.

I would like to start with the most common perspective, namely when there is real, often sexual, physical abuse. The most significant legacy of such abuse is an excess of stimulation and sensoriality that clogs up the mind and alters some of its basic functions, notably a person's fundamental trust in caregivers and adults. Bullying – in other words, when older children abuse, rape or humiliate a designated victim – is another important type of phenomenon. Any number of examples can be found in films or books. There is another type I would like to add, which I generally break down into three subtypes:

* *The dead mother*. Admirably described by André Green (1983), the depressed mother is incapable of accepting or metabolizing the beta elements evacuated by the child in her care.

- *Spoilt children.* This is a topic dear to Franco Borgogno. An excess of anxiety, care and catastrophic alarms prevents children who feel unable to live through conflict, independence and adulthood from developing "emotional legs".

Snakes

In her relationship with her mother Marina is an "I'll be what you want me to be" type of girl. One day she comes across "a snake" on a mountain path and from then on, she no longer dares to leave the house.

At your bidding

Luciana lives within the orbit of her parents and is unable to attain independence. In a recurring dream *she is with her mother in a luxury hotel. Unable to put on her own clothes, she has to wear those of her mother* (in other words, "as you want me to be"). In the next dream *she wants to go to Amsterdam* (transgression, independence) *but her parents talk her out of it for fear of terrorist attacks.* Then again in the following dream a killer (equivalent to the "snake" for the other patient) *breaks into the house but she manages to escape to safety by taking refuge in a bathtub filled with sweets.* Symbiosis – the sweets – is what protects her from any violent experience of separation.

Oblomov, the couch potato

After six years of analysis, Carla enters the hall in my studio as she has many times before and, with an air of amazement, says: "Ah, there's a couch. Has it always been there?"

Obviously, it has, but she had never considered her Oblomov-couch potato! In fact, even though she is approaching 40 and has still not managed to free herself from her family ties/straps,[1] being the "good girl" she is, Carla loves to rest on her laurels.

- *Negative reverie.* This is a well-known concept that was initially described as a reversal of the flow of projective identifications (Ferro, 1987).

We can incorporate these latter aspects into a composition where violent aspects abuse fragile aspects.

Reality

A question many analysts often raise concerns the relationship between reality and a patient's communication. This is a problem that has already been solved by anyone who has explored Kleinian thought in any depth: internal reality is as real as external reality. Internal reality constitutes a kind of parallel world, *a world within*, that is as true as the external world. The same goes for the "reality of the field".

Aldo Costa – an analyst active in Palermo at the time of Alexandra Tomasi, Princess of Lampedusa – firmly declared that the analyst must come to terms with the "mourning" of reality.

Of course, this depends on the context in which he or she works.

Communications made in a living room during conversations with friends convey clear and realistic meanings, and "the analyst in the living room" or "the analyst on the train" is not an analyst but a human being using everyday codes of communication.

When the context becomes the consulting room – and if a setting is also in place and operative – that is where "the analyst" really does come to life. The context becomes the analytic context – where the multi-dimensional, multi-virtual space of the field is brought to life.

In the field we perform the following operations:

DE-CONCRETIZATION

ONEIRIZATION

DE-CONSTRUCTION

RE-DREAMING

If a patient tells us he was abused by his uncle when he was a child, or that he has recently been operated on for a benign lung tumour, it would obviously be wrong not to adhere to the "true reality" of his story. But if the context for this communication is a consulting room, there is good reason to open ourselves up to other possible meanings. These are not to be interpreted immediately – that would be madness – but they will begin to take up residence in our mind and therefore in the field we have generated with the patient. For example: one idea we might want to open up to is that among the many potential identities that come to life in the field there is also an abusive and violent (psychotic?) "function". We might also come to realize that our interest should be focused more on the possibility of management/transformation than on trauma.

Later, the patient dreams of *living in a building where the concierge reads pornographic magazines and being afraid that his teenage daughter might be exposed to such magazines.*

Then he talks about a high-spirited young boy in the same class as his youngest son. After that he goes back to *the dream in which there seemed to be a "foreign alter ego", one that was oriental or, to be more precise, Indian.*

It seems to me that there are multiple possible modes of intervention. For example, some might be more interpretive in nature (that is to say, are organized according to a notion of *the unconscious as something that is already given and needs to be deciphered*): so excitatory defence against depressed aspects, explosive incontinence, and also a part that is foreign or alien that he experiences as living inside him.

Or alternatively, going according to the notion of *the unconscious as something to be built*, one could proceed by gradually weaving narrative transformations that spring from reverie. After all, it is better for the concierge to read a pornographic magazine than for him to get depressed and not do his job well. One could go on to point out that there seem to be more bison in the classroom than fences to contain them, and finally one could say that the oriental person perceived as an alien might be someone selling the Kamasutra in the west. The question would then be how much space to give him.

Pearls of insanity

Emotional management and digestion

We have always maintained that behind anorexia (or bulimia) lies an ecographic image of things that is deeper and more complete than the normal gaze: that is to say, what we are dealing with in this case is not a disperception but rather an emotional "hyperperception". It is as if anorexics or bulimics had a sort of Hound of the Baskervilles inside them that needs to be kept under control either through a strategy of starvation (turning the hound into a chihuahua) or by sleep-inducing overeating.

The next step may be to consider that the hound can also represent other emotions in their pure state or amalgamated with each other. In Giovanni's case, the hound is the embodiment of his significant depressive state.

Starving the hound is one possible strategy for coping with "hound depression". By the same token, we might regard the hound (with its often lacerating bites of depression) as made up of a shoal of piraña. Then deconstructing depression – or this Lego-style depression – "into small pieces" would be the way to metabolize the Lego-like sub-units of loneliness, abandonment, anger, despair. . . .

Giulio and the goldfish

At the beginning of his analysis Giulio recounts a dream in which he approached *a girl and then a blade appeared; blood then flowed from the girl's slashed open belly*. There are many possible interventions. I choose one: "Might there have been a Jack the Ripper?" The patient replies: "I remember going to see the Alcantara Gorge, and in a rock pool there was a goldfish that was gasping for air because it was in saltwater and not in freshwater; then it was also torn apart by the sharp rocks".

The interpretation I gave that brought Jack the Ripper on stage, as it were, was oversalted. The patient had imagined a beginning that was softer and not so sharp-edged, and his swift cutting intervention communicated his feeling of having been torn open. Probably what is required is a "sweeter/gentler ecosystem" (the Italian expression for freshwater is "sweet water", or *dolce acqua*) where goldfish no longer come to harm.

Psychotherapy and psychoanalysis

I would like to present an example to illustrate the difference between psychotherapy and psychoanalysis. The former remains tied to the concreteness of the communication, while the latter is above all an act of "mourning of reality".

If a patient were to explain that part of his work involved using a metal detector to detect bombs and weapons, and then went on to describe how when he was 9 years old his mother had told him in the presence of his brother that she was not his real mother and that he was the son of his supposed mother's sister, who had died in childbirth, and that ever since then he has felt anger and resentment, there would be two paths we could take.

The path of psychotherapy: this would mean staying within the dramatic and traumatic concreteness of this narrative, going back over its various stages, suffering, finding possible adjustments and processing the trauma.

The path of psychoanalysis (actually I should use the word in the plural because very much depends on the different fields that can be activated):

the patient has found a narrative that allows him to share his "drama". He is filled with furious, explosive rage, which he must continually keep in check, having at some point realized that his mother had been a *dead mother*, that is, a mother without reverie (R; or with -R) even though it was true that to one half she had been a present and functioning mother – the part of himself called "brother".

The story is a vehicle that conveys deep and as yet unknown realities.

We may suppose that this will become the subtext of the analysis until life is restored to the mother who had functioned depressively with him; hence his indigestible anger and hatred still in search for an Author and Characters.

The dead mother would then be the character who enables us to talk about the depressed and non-functioning part of the living mother.

Defence mechanisms of depression

In one of his articles, Pichon-Rivière (1971) states that depression is the basic disease from which the other forms of mental suffering differ and develop. The most frequent defences are of the excitatory type. Excitement is experienced as the opposite of depression, but in actual fact it simply masks depression and negates it without ever allowing it to be metabolized.

In recent years the prime defence mechanism is that which is connected to eroticization. This ranges from flagrant forms of hypersexuality (nymphomania) to frequenting sex clubs, free love, and even the more subtle forms of compulsive flirting. It now also includes age groups previously immune from these phenomena, as seen in the growing phenomenon of cougars, milfs and even gilfs. Male versions are obviously also available.

Eroticization as a defence against depression

A 56-year-old woman treats her depression by having sexual relations with her fellow teachers and with the young men she teaches, and also by going around dressed up in a titillating and provocative way, wearing high heels and slits that make her an object of desire despite her age. She flirts with every man who approaches her and afterwards tells her husband what it's possible to tell. In this way she creates an eroticized field full of excitement, which in both of them counteracts the depression associated with the passage of time and its inevitable one-way linearity.

This is a kind of "multifocal and multi-temporal Professor Unrat syndrome": every place becomes somewhere to eroticize and every age has its places. From Internet dating to provocative ways of dressing.

For another patient, eroticization was not an end in itself but served to create a field of excitement through the quarrels that jealousy triggered between her and her partner.

In his first sessions, a university professor described going to a sex club where he found himself being embraced by a "well-hung black guy". This marks the entry on the scene of the "black man of his denied depression" with an enormous penis; the penis is also the enormous "pains"[2] he has finally been able to get into contact with despite trying to shake them off by means of excitement.

A woman pharmacist, now getting on in years but who dresses in an eye-catching way, has attracted an entourage of admirers who bombard her with phone calls and proposals. She has managed to make these conquests at the counter in the pharmacy where she works by virtue of her forward manner and way of dressing. Another woman well past middle age has specialized in seducing shop assistants in big-city stores where she goes "commando-style" to "try on clothes". The result is that she has even had some nasty adventures with men who felt entitled to make all kinds of advances, along the lines of "sleep with me and I'll buy you lunch".

Another 58-year-old is known as the "hoochie-coochie woman" because of her habit of going to discos, where she lets her hair down at weekends; then there are also so-called "cougars" and "dog walkers", who "offer themselves for sex to others frequenting the places where people take their dogs for a walk".

Then there was another woman whose speciality was seducing her children's teachers and hard-up immigrants struggling with real-life difficulties. For her, the excitement was double or triple: it was in itself erotic, it gave her thrill of being pursued, with the added more subtle danger of catching a disease. Often relationships with younger women become the putative medicine against the anguish caused by the passage of time. I have focused on these modalities because they are the most frequent in our current culture.

Others that perform the same function include:

- Sadomasochistic relationships;
- Gambling;

- Drug use;
- Dangerous or extreme sports.

And so on and so forth – both in the literal and metaphorical sense.

Of course, there are also any number of possible interconnected mechanisms that can be exchanged and reciprocated indefinitely. A depressed woman, a high school teacher, used to chat away with a young male colleague while correcting her pupils' homework and drinking at the same time. In this way she eroticized the situation to the point where the colleague became her stalker. The situation exploded when the husband found out about it and told the young colleague's wife, which provoked an all-round high-temperature antidepressant uproar.

This same teacher would occasionally make cryptic remarks to her husband ("sometimes at work one gets involved with colleagues and it's difficult to get out of it") suggesting that the inevitable had happened. Eventually the husband exploded with all the jealousy and feelings of suspicion that had been set off inside him; the main thing, however, was that the goal of raising the temperature had been achieved.

When countered using such methods, depression does not diminish; indeed, increasing doses of "therapy" become necessary. It is as if someone were to take painkillers to treat an "acute abdominal pain". The symptom disappears but at the cost of masking the cause of the pathology. Sometimes it is the brush with reality – an impossible "O" – that forces the individual to make contact with the depressive wound.

As pointed out earlier, the possible prototype of depressive situations is Green's "dead mother" – a mentally dead mother who is unable to receive or to metabolize anguish and thus cannot pass on the method for such metabolization. This causes a reactive anger that in turn is on the lookout for a mind (and an alpha function that knows how to receive and transform it). A possible metaphor for this would be someone throwing a red-hot boomerang (uncontainable fiery emotions) that might do one of two things:

- It might strike and be "caught" by the kangaroo that cools it down and manages it;
- Or it may not find the kangaroo (the other person's mind that is capable of dealing with the boomerang by using "tools for thinking").

And then it comes back even hotter than before and full of kinetic energy and hits the thrower.

In other words, depression results from unaccepted and unmetabolized beta proto-emotions that invade the sender or failed evacuator.

I think it should be clear to everyone that depression as a state of mental suffering has nothing to do with the depressive position, which denotes a state of mental integration.

It would, however, perhaps be useful to describe "tools for thinking":

- The first tool is the alpha function or that "something" that is capable of absorbing sensoriality by transforming it into pictograms or proto-images, sequences of which form "waking dream thought".

Other *tools* are:

- The PS ↔ D oscillation, to which I would add the contiguous autistic position (ACP). So, there are at least three basic configurations of the mind: autistic, paranoid-schizoid and depressive. Nuclei of these ways of functioning are omnipresent. When one of them dominates, a configuration comes into being that corresponds to a type of psychic suffering.
- Negative capability ↔ selected fact oscillation.
- The container/contained relationship.
- The function of alignment or attunement between minds that produces *unison*.

When they operate syncretically, these functions could be called "capacity for reverie".

The relationship and the field

These are two very different concepts. The former involves two people, the latter a group; the former is narrow, the latter expansive; the former is claustrophobic, the latter agoraphiliac. In the relationship, the concreteness and reality of the characters are more important. What applies in the field is the principle of the loss and deconstruction of reality.

Just as the characters in the former are factual, in the latter they are theatrical. One way of putting it is to say that the former partakes of Socialist Realism and the latter of Pirandello and Chagall.

From a relational perspective, the figures summoned up in the session are people who interact with each other and form bonds. From a field point of view, the "characters" are functions of minds waiting for a gestalt to break up, and which once it is transformed comes together again and so on. The kind of psychoanalysis that reconstructs psychosexual and childhood development is replaced by one that develops tools for thinking. In terms of an orchestra, the concept of relationship would relate to the ever more pitch-perfect execution of the score, while the concept of the field would suggest an experimental orchestra desirous of creating new instruments and exploring even further the potential of those already known.

The pink bison

A patient talks about *a dream in which a pink bison pops up behind him. At first the bison terrified him with its blackness, but now he was less afraid and he even felt like smiling.*

"The pink bison makes me think more of a soft toy", I say, and this triggers a series of memories of the games he used to play as a child. These are obviously a way of talking about what he is doing today (now), and how he is playing with and mixing together emotions and affects.

"Concrete" communication

The transvestite

A patient describes how once when he was on call, he had to section a transsexual suffering from a full-blown manic episode.

A session follows in which various dreams are worked through.

The session also offers me the opportunity to find a way of coming back to the figure of the transsexual.

I make the point that perhaps he has always put the emphasis on duty, study, work and left little room for fun, pleasure, or to put it another way the small quotient of carnival that might find space in life.

The patient welcomes this latest Lego brick, linking it up to a series of interventions that expand the field of the dialectic between the rationality that boxes him in and the emotionality he fears might spill out.

He starts the next day's session by talking about the excessively serious atmosphere that had always reigned at his home. When his grandfather Giovanni had given him a moped and a PlayStation console as presents, his parents had sent them back. He then describes other episodes marked by seriousness and earnestness. Towards the end of the session, I put forward several examples to make the point that his life recipe should prescribe more spoonfuls of grandfather Giovanni – not just one, but even three or four. I also point out that the limbic system has rights of its own, including the right to consolation, so that he is not left in the limbo of reason.

The knock

At the beginning of the session, Amelia talks about the concern she had felt when she had phoned home at lunchtime and was told by the baby-minder that her 3-year-old son had thrown himself backwards off a chair and banged his head violently. Fortunately, the knock he had taken had had no alarming consequences.

She then goes on to inundate the session with stories about today and the day before, explaining that she realizes that if she talks less the child speaks more.

I tell her that it is good that she feels she can talk about lots of things but that sometimes the child's most emotional, most intimate voice is drowned out (as if many things were being sealed away). She adds: "By saying so many things, I stop you from hearing the most intimate things that get mixed up with all my other communications".

De-concretization

I would now like to try setting the de-concretization gauge to the highest level and introduce the concept of "dream organizer", something that originates in a good oscillation between NC and SF (negative capability and selected fact).

Fruit and vegetables

A patient talks about working for a family-run fruit-and-vegetable company, and describes the difficult situation she has been in since some friends and some members of her family had begun to fall ill and to suffer more and more. Moreover, suddenly out of the blue she had reached the age of 54 almost without realizing it.

Immediately I see "fruit and vegetables" as a dream organizer, or rather the dream I have about the patient is about a "vegetarian" who at a certain point is contaminated by contact with "the flesh/meat", in other words, with the suffering of the flesh and the human condition in general. She then begins to de-artichoke, or de-carotize, or de-lemonize and has now taken on within herself human attributes such as awareness of the passing of time and of the prospect of death.

This long journey from the plant world to the animal and human world will be the starting point of her analysis if it is shared and developed by the dream that is activated within the patient, or rather within the shared dream field.

Fertilizations

A patient requests an analysis, explaining about all the deaths and illnesses that have been troubling her family for some time. Things are not looking good; not even the "artificial insemination" treatment has produced results. Here too I could take the "dream organizer" path but I prefer to follow a path that is easier to share and less intuitive, namely, to look at the basic model that determines how waking dream thought is formed.

Pictogram	Pictogram	Pictogram
↓	↓	↓
Narrative derivative 1	Narrative derivative 2	Narrative derivative 3

Let us imagine another possible narrative derivative of the same sequence of pictograms: "A gardener came to me for advice, complaining that nothing was growing in his garden, that plants and flowers dried up and that nothing he sowed ever took root, not even the seeds his neighbour had given him that he had taken from his own thriving garden". The dream, or the *fabula*, is exactly the same; the only thing that changes is the *syuzhet*.

Or again we could talk about an auto electrician who complained that the battery he had just bought goes flat straight away and stays flat no matter how often he recharges it. De-concretizing, forgoing the real, opens the door to a kind of psychoanalysis that is about developing tools for thinking and not about discovering altogether interchangeable contents.

And while the tears triggered by different situations of abuse may vary, the dream is still about contents that "abuse" inadequate containers.

The baby that is not yet a chick

Now in her third year of analysis, Marianna talks with great concern about her 3-year-old son who hardly speaks. She never calls him by name but uses an incredible number of terms of endearment, long expressions brimming with overabundant tenderness (by the by, the expressions she uses include "mum's sole reason for joy and life", "mum's infinite and limitless love", "the reason for my happiness", "beautiful treasure" and so on). A few days earlier she had been in a bookshop with her child when a man asked him: "What's your name?", to which Lorenzo replied: "Egg"!

This is the episode that brings up the fact that the mother never used to call her child by name. He could be Luigi or Carlo or Stefano and has no individuality of his own; he is just his mother's accessory. I cannot stop myself from making a remark I am sure the patient will understand. I say: "There is a smell in the air of mother from Cogne!"[3]

Transformations into dreams

The town that is not yet a ghost

During a supervision, a young analyst tells me about a patient she describes as "extremely concrete" who she can never get anything out of. He had been to Amsterdam and told her the whole story of his trip: the different areas of the city, the redlight district, the courtyard of the Beguines, the aquarium built mostly underwater, the coffee shops where you can buy hashish. . . .

Nobody has taught her about "narrative deconstruction", which would open the door to new meanings. If only she prefaced the beginning of the story with the words "I had a dream in which . . . I went to Amsterdam", she would understand that it is her listening that is concrete, not the story told by the patient. He does his job by telling her about his inner city, with its mental neighbourhoods, its inhabitants, its depression, its manic defences and much more. . . .

The analyst rests

A supervisee recounts a session that she had experienced as not tiring because the patient did not say anything significant. Occasionally, she adds, you need the occasional session like that to take a rest.

The patient had spoken about various things: a doctorate he was planning to do, a friend who shows absolutely no interest in him, "who now just couldn't give a shit about him", the hard work he has to do on his thesis, and lastly, he recounts a dream: his girlfriend took off her blouse to shave her armpits, while another couple watched on in amazement. This seems to be a concrete session, but using the magical filter of "I had a dream in which . . ." we feel the desire to explore in more depth what the patient was really saying, to dispel his fear that the analyst is not interested in him, that he does not pay attention to him or consider him. The consulting room has transformed into a beauty salon where the analyst just wants to "chill out". It is obvious that all this may follow different paths from those of relational explication and "playing in the body".

The Serb in the harem

A patient describes taking a psychological test at a fairground which showed that his brain was almost 100 per cent female. I feel something inside me that makes me suspicious: this something comes to life when he talks about a terrible, violent and unscrupulous Serb who after a series of coincidences is now living at his parents' house. What better place is there than a harem to hide a violent man?

The preverbal and the O-3 in the session

Giulio is having an extramarital affair with Barbara, a young trainee he has met at the law firm where he works.

After one of his dreams, we worked for a long time on the "absinthe" effect that women have on him. This is followed by the period during which we work on Barbara as an antidepressant that also has side effects.

In one session, Barbara's parents appear. After discovering their daughter's relationship with a man twice her age, they tell her: "You'll end up having to be his caregiver, changing his incontinence pads . . .". During the same session the patient talked about how he had recently looked after her when she had intestinal flu – being there for her when she vomited, changing her, washing her.

Here it is clear to me that the quotient of antidepressant and pain-killing eroticism was only one part. The resistant fulcrum of their bond, the steel wire rope that bound them together consisted precisely in this looking after and being looked after, this mutual changing of nappies.

It was perhaps time to start giving up this need for primary care and grow up. Therapy (taking care) is not about words or interpretation but is rather a matter of creating a "pampering/pampers-like" field that makes it possible to experience something that first has to be made reality and lived through before it is given up.

Mara (1), Mara (2), Merkel and the Turks

The same happens with Mara (1) who falls madly in love with another Mara because Mara (2) had uttered "I want you" – something she had always missed.

The "I want you" field will have to come to life also via Merkel and the Turkish immigrants, who in turn will need to experience being really wanted: only if I feel you want me can I agree to grow.

Notes

1 In Italian there is an untranslatable play on words: "ties" is "legami", which can be broken down into "leg-*ami*" or "love (*tu ami* = you love) that binds" or "*lega-mi[nacc]i*" (i.e., "ties that pose a threat").
2 In Italian, the singular of the word for penis is a homograph of the plural of the word "pain".
3 This is a reference to a tragic fact of infanticide by the mother that happened in Cogne, a little town in Val d'Aosta.

References

Burger, N. (Director) (2014). *Divergent*. USA.

Ferro, A. (1987). Il mondo alla rovescia. *Rivista di Psicoanalisi*, 33:59–77.

Green, A. (1983). *Life Narcissism, Death Narcissism*. London: Free Association Books, 2001.

Pichon-Rivière, E. (1971). *La psiquiatría. Une nueva problemítica. Del psicoanálisis a la psicología social*. Buenos Aires: Nueva Visión.

Chapter VI

The birth of the psyche and intercorporeity

First, let's consider two famous Madonna and Child classical paintings. The first one is the *Madonna and Child* by the "Master of the Strauss Madonna",[1] now at the Museum of Fine Arts, Houston. I saw it recently in Rome at Palazzo Barberini. I was intrigued and surprised by the gaze that mother and child exchange.

The mother's eyes express her knowledge of the fatal destiny of the child, but I gave myself the liberty of imagining something else: that, on the contrary, staying with a lay interpretation, it reflected more her distress, sadness and anger (see Winnicott [1949] and the seventeen reasons a mother has to hate her baby).

Now, let's now reflect upon the painting by Filippo Lippi, Virgin with Child (1466–1469), in Palazzo Medici-Riccardi, Florence. What is curious about it is that – unlike the many paintings that have the same subject as the so-called "sacred conversation", or scenes of children held in mother's arms, or breastfeeding, or staring at their mother's eyes – here, mother and child are ecstatically lost in tactile contact, cheek to cheek, or, rather, skin to skin. This is a contact that does not rest on the need for nutrition. Lippi's masterpiece perfectly illustrates Ogden's (1994) hypothesis regarding the place where the first glimmer of subjectivity and, therefore, of relationality is born in the child: in the area where the child's cheek is in contact with the mother's breast, starting from the sensation of the calming quality that is produced there.

This is not always an easy point to grasp. As human beings, we come from the night of our animality or, depending on the point of view, from the Eden of our animality. But, since we became human, or speaking beings, when a child is born and grows up in a human community, the child is immediately taken into the network of the symbolic – in fact, from even

DOI: 10.4324/9781003279020-6

before birth (Lacan, 1966/2006). At the beginning of his life, an infant receives his impressions through various sensory channels in the form of sensations organized in rhythmic patterns. After all, this is the idea of Original Sin.

From the very moment of conception, the child is already in sin, and sin presupposes self-awareness. The first dimension of *sense*, rather than *meaning*, therefore has to do with primitive sensations and emotions that are generated by areas of overlap in the experience lived between mother and child of attunement or unison. These sensations and emotions bring order and help to establish a primordial concept of self.

For this reason, the *Virgin and Child* by Lippi lends itself to illustrate better than other similar images. Bion's (1970) concept of *at-one-ment* as the agent of psychic containment, which means both unison and expiation ("atonement"). If there is something to atone for, if every time it is necessary to reconcile with the divine (i.e., with the object and through it metonymically with the wider sociality), it means that there is always a virtual state of conflict. By unison/*at-one-ment*, we can then understand a *dialectical* process of identity and difference. At the beginning of life, the first concepts could more appropriately be called *habits, bodily concepts/ schemes* or *sensory ideas* that correspond to the progressive sedimentation of implicit or procedural memories. Then we come to the representations and concepts themselves, but these never supplant the emotional-sensory ones (could they be called "emotional pictograms"?).

One of Kant's phrases that Bion (for example, 1977/1991) often mentions is that concepts without perceptions are empty, and perceptions without concepts are blind. But, in other points, he says that compared to psychic reality, emotions are perceptions directed inwards – that is to say, they perform the same function that the perceptions of the senses perform for the objects of the external world. Therefore, a functioning mind can never be made only by perceptions or only by concepts because, in order to be human, we need both. But neither can it be made only by external perceptions because without the internal perceptions represented by emotions, one would live like the Viscount of Italo Calvino (1952/1998): halved, lost in the sea of concreteness, in hallucinosis, with a vision of the world in black and white.

As with external perceptions, "affective" perceptions must bring grain to the mill of that mediating function between senses and intellect that is called imagination. Only afterwards, the apparatus for thinking thoughts can synthesize the multiplicity of all this mass of data in the unity of the concept. In philosophy, an author who tries to go deeper into the functioning of the imagination (of the alpha function?) is Fichte (1794). He sharply describes the imagination as a psychic activity that oscillates from one thing to its opposite and from one side to the opposite side, as if it revolves around us, comparing various perspectives that it then makes available to the intellect for conceptual synthesis. His discourse surprises us because it seems that he is describing the great richness and productivity of the ambiguity of dreams and poetry.

The body exists as a "corporeal subject" – it has its own motor intentionality, it knows and "understands" the world in its own way – that is, it has a practical or procedural knowledge of it (*praktognosia*). If it has an intentionality, it means that then the body moves *towards* something or moves *away* from it and therefore organizes a spatiality and determines behaviours. This understanding of the world is made up of bodily patterns as Schilder (1950) described them: "systems", "totality", dynamic "fields" of sensory impressions otherwise dispersed, fantasies in the body (Gaddini, 1982). We therefore have a clear intentionality, but one which can also be unconscious and therefore latent, and an intentionality by its nature opaque because it cannot be translated exactly into words and concepts. If we want to avoid separating the psyche from the body, we have to think that in the human dimension – in the realm of the symbolic – the different forms of intentionality influence each other and are part of the same field. This is why it can be said that the subject begins to exist in the sacred conversation of the cheek-breast contact and that this is the area in which the psyche gradually settles.

It goes without saying that if it is "sacred", it means that, at the origin of the bond between mother and child (of the birth of the psyche), there is the intervention of the Spirit, but a Spirit that here we define, with Hegel, not as a metaphysical entity but as "a fundamental *relation* among persons that mediates their *self-consciousness*, a way in which people reflect on what they have come to take as authoritative for themselves" (Pinkard, 1996, p. 9). It is not correct, therefore, to think of bodily intentionality as a purely *natural* intentionality because it is impregnated from the beginning, at the birth of each individual, by culture or sociality. The spatiality organized by bodily intentionality can therefore be defined as a *human* spatiality. To know anything is to *recognize* each other as subjects and to share a belonging to the intersubjective field of human sociality characterized by the use of language. It means to awaken each time to something new because even what seems not new or simply transmitted from one to the other is always inscribed in a new and ever-changing context.

In light of what I have said so far, the relationship between minds can then be seen as the ongoing negotiation between individuals of sense and meaning – in essence, of the mutual emotional distance and the status of person (*persona*, in ancient Roman, means the mask used by actors) that pertains to each. The way in which we define socially the "mask", which is in continuous transformation, and that we are allowed to wear, passes through several channels and is not perfectly controllable precisely because each subject is only a node of the infinite network that connects all human beings in the *medium* of language. Paradoxically, to become a subject or *finite* being in the sense of having stable boundaries – a psychic skin – the infant passes through the widest possible absorption of this *infinite*. The more we are human and feel to exist authentically, feel to be real, the more perspectives we have on the reality of things and of ourselves, and, therefore, the more we become *infinite*. With Nietzsche (1995), we obey the urge both to become who we are and to become "gods"/divines. Even in Christianity, the events of the Cross tell the story of the incarnation of the divine infinity of language in the human finite of Jesus, and then the resurrection or, rather, the ascent from the (animal) materiality of the body to the Spirit – in fact, an incessant coming and going, a dialectical trade between the non-vitality of the anatomical body and the vitality of the lived body. In other words, the relationship between minds (but here "mind" also stands for the human being who expresses himself or herself *through* and *in* the body) consists of the fact of being elements in the field of language, of inhabiting the place where sense and meaning are generated.

This is why the only "drive" that Bion is interested in, as it is relevant to the field of psychoanalysis, is the emotional drive or what Grotstein (2004) calls the "truth drive": because it is now the concept of a drive no longer minimally compromised with any *direct* somatic causality. What do I mean? That it is *sociality* that pushes the individual to differentiate more and more and to reach the highest possible degree of consensuality – a dimension that, moreover, does not exclude the possibility of conflict; conflict is certainly not its antithesis. The drive, in the classical sense, originates from the body; the truth drive originates from the group. And, even when the drive becomes desire, in Freud, the theoretical aspect is that it is desire of the other in view of instinctual satisfaction, not desire for truth. While in Bion, the drive for truth translates to the thirst for relationship. From this point of view, psychic suffering is, therefore, what marks the condition of the individual who is outside of consensuality – that is, outside of the possibility of attributing a full and personal sense, but at the same time also *impersonal*, to the individual's own life experience – not only in the case of psychosis, but always and everywhere. The relationship between minds is a mutual influence under the pressure of an impulse to differentiate that has an obvious adaptive value.

Now, to try to see at an even more molecular level what the relationship consists of that is properly psychic but also intercorporeal between two subjects, and, in particular, the intimate dialectic of identity and difference that, as we have seen, characterizes it, I propose to look at another beautiful image: the painting by Simone Vouet, *Psyché et l'amour* (*Cupid and Psyche*, 1626–1629), now at the Musée des Beaux-Arts de Lyon, which illustrates the key moment of the fable of Apuleius's *Cupid and Psyche* (2006).

Eros and psyche

The fairy tale of *Eros and Psyche*, taken from the *Metamorphoses* of Apuleius, a Latin writer of the second century AD, focuses precisely on psychic transformations in allegorical form. The protagonist, Psyche, arouses the envy of Venus for her beauty. The goddess then orders her son Eros (or Cupid) to make Psyche fall in love with the ugliest of men. But, instead, Eros himself falls in love with her and welcomes her in his beautiful palace (a figure of the Ego?). Here, Psyche is served by handmaids whom she cannot see. She can only hear their voices (does not any name have a hallucinatory character insofar as it necessarily "abstracts" from the concreteness of the thing itself?). But, every night she experiences voluptuousness by joining (an act that we can interpret as the instance of unison in the relationship) with her husband. The pact, however, is that *everything has to happen in the dark*. In fact, when she transgresses the prohibition and, while holding a knife in one hand, projects some light and looks at her lover's body, she is thrown out of the palace. What does it mean?

Among the many possible meanings, a psychoanalytic reading could recognize in this story a version of the aesthetic conflict. It is interesting that, unlike the Meltzerian scheme, here, the sense through which the object is positively perceived as seductive is not *sight* but *touch*, while the negative – what scares – is represented by what is not visible. Evidently Psyche, the mind, if it is to stay alive, needs to remain in relationship through the other with the sacredness of language and with the community. Perhaps, the developing psyche needs to be, at the same time, in proximity to *and* also at a certain distance from the object. And the object can only oscillate between the two poles of being an absent presence or a present absence, "the place where the breast used to be" and where it is no longer, even if it keeps its mark, not a *naughtness* but a *ni-ente* (not-being), or a not-thing.

What the fairy tale suggests is that a mind can develop only if its need for love is satisfied. When the anti-libidinal impulse of envy prevails – a sentiment that always reveals a dramatic lack of some vital element – the subject risks falling into the abyss of depression (abandoned by Eros as a result of the harmful curiosity instilled in her by the envy of her sisters, Psyche almost kills herself several times). Finally, voluptuousness (pleasure) comes from Eros and not vice versa – as if to say that for human beings, "tenderness" is the fruit of mutual recognition (paraphrasing Freud, a pleasure of a different kind?). It is more important for the subject of the sexual discharge that it comes *before* the direct drive satisfaction. In Winnicott's terms, the needs of the Ego are ahead of those of the *Es* (Id).

Psyche's desire to see Eros is thus the same as the child's desire to know what is in the mother's head (or body) – that is to say, to arrive at possessing the object entirely, to transform the invisible into visible. This is not possible because the subject can exist as such only if the subject renounces this possession – in the same way in which, for example, we must accept the relative "loss" of reality that occurs in the use of the concept. Allegorically, becoming a subject means learning to tolerate not seeing the body of Eros (it is not by chance that he is of divine nature, and it is significant that "divinity" is for Bion one of the names of O, of the unknowable) and, therefore, also running the risk that in the end, the invisibility of the other may turn out to be "monstrous".

So, in the psychoanalytic theorization of the Oedipus, what becomes the nakedness of the mother (the incest) is just another figure of the necessary opacity of her mind in the eyes of the infant and the invisibility of O, with respect to the cognitive faculty of the subject. If this frontier is violated, terrible things happen: *one loses one's head*. For Kristeva (1980/1982), the abject of the mother's body is this monstrous one from which one must separate (i.e., not see, keep in the dark), in order to be born as an individual. If the pact is respected, *voluptas* is born (but not yet Voluptas, as the divine daughter of Psyche and Eros, which is counted among the minor deities called Personifications or Abstractions), at the same time as pleasure and the desire for pleasure is born.

As we can see, Psyche – the mind, the access to the primary and secondary symbolization, in essence the establishment of the primary relationship and the ego – has to do with a certain game of visible and invisible, of presence and absence of the object, of a certain simultaneous and paradoxical disappearance and reappearance. In itself, the sign, the symbol, the word, the name are the agents responsible for regulating this game. As Žižek (1989/2009) writes,

> as soon as the reality is symbolized, caught in a symbolic network, the thing itself is more present in a word, in its concept, than its immediate physical reality. More precisely, we cannot return to the immediate reality: even if we turn from the word to the thing – from the word "table" to the table in its physical reality, for example – the appearance of the table itself is already marked with a certain lack – to know what a table really is, what it means, we must have recourse to the word which implies an absence of the thing.
>
> (p. 131)

In a relationship, the tolerance of darkness (of frustration) is the alchemical element that together with Eros gives birth to Psyche.

That the key scenes of the relationship between Eros and Psyche are, therefore, all played out in the dimension of tactile and acoustic is a detail not without meaning. On the level of the signifier, it evokes the sound and body quality; but, on the level of the meaning, it evokes the incorporeal quality of the word (of thought and conscience) – or, better, of a corporeity "reduced" to sound, "without the presence of anyone", exactly as incorporeal is representation (*Vorstellung*). The sound of the word only gives us a relative permanence of the thing and otherwise exposes us to the frustration of absence. The monstrosity that Psyche fears to discover in her husband is thus a figure of the absence, necessary and relative, of *any* object. The love of Eros (of the object) can only be had if we tolerate the frustration inherent in not being able to possess it entirely. In the fable, therefore, the prohibition of seeing the face of the divine (of

"God") and the transgression of the prohibition are central. In essence, one must have faith that, in the mind of the object, there is no "malevolent" intention. This is the essence of the aesthetic conflict. If, on the other hand, the curiosity aroused by envy has the upper hand, it is bound to lead to the *sacrilega curiositas* (profane curiosity), to the arrogant action (*hýbris*) that does not comply with the laws. Then, you are going to face a disastrous fate.

Why is it "disastrous" if, in the fairy tale, the passion that Psyche arouses in Eros repeatedly saves her from envy and depression, and leads her to the happy ending of the wedding? But what happens in this ending? Psyche is assumed into heaven among the gods and then *stops being human*. For this reason, I would say that it is only a seemingly happy ending (and, in the end, even if we read this last episode of the story as the allegory of a loss in the emptiness of pure abstraction of thought). It is true, there is a reunion and, as we said, from the two is born Voluptas. But only until she was human could Psyche be loved by Eros and stay in his beautiful palace, albeit at a certain price – at the price of *not seeing* him.

Orpheus and Eurydice

There is another myth where something similar happens, which seems like a variation on the Eros and Psyche fable by Apuleius. In the myth of Orpheus, there is an analogous prohibition to turn to contemplate the face of the beloved redeemed from Hades through the art of singing, and an analogous transgression with an end – this time, openly inauspicious. A further analogy could be between the desire to see something that cannot be seen – the thoughts of the mother, Eros, or Eurydice – and the impulse to want to dominate the infinite "divine" of the unconscious as language. An allusion to Orpheus and Eurydice could then be seen in the episode, *mise en abîme* of the main plot, of Psyche going to the Underworld by order of Venus and breaking the prohibition to open a box that would contain some of the beauty of Proserpine.

The fact is that – apart from the two different endings, respectively, of Apuleius's fable and of the myth narrated by Ovid (2008) – the transgression of the prohibition to see (perhaps, better, to know perfectly: *theoréin* means "to see") the beloved face provokes a catastrophe. We know superficially what determines the one and the other to it: fear, envy – the sisters can be thought of as her own impulses – and curiosity in Psyche, and impatience in Orpheus and his great desire for Eurydice. In fact, if we ask ourselves, in conclusion, what it is that Psyche loses, we read from Apuleius that a thousand emotions of her calamity drag her here and there.

In this regard, the commentators have continued to make all kinds of assumptions. In closing, I would like to provide an explanation that seems to me to enlighten the particular perspective with which we are considering these classics of universal culture. In the case of Orpheus, the impulse would be determined by the awareness, which comes at a certain point, that in Eurydice there can no longer be anything alive. Orpheus's gesture would no longer be tantamount to failing to mourn and, therefore, to tolerating the absence of the object, but, on the contrary, he would have realized the emptiness of his undertaking and would have *chosen* to make her disappear.

This is how he would be able to mourn his beloved. This interpretation is due to Rilke, and is found in his poem "Orpheus Eurydice Hermes" (1907). When Orpheus turns around, Hermes, aggrieved, communicates it to Eurydice, who at first does not understand.

> And when suddenly the god
> held her back and with a voice of pain
> pronounced the words: He has turned away –
> she did not understand, and said softly: *Who*?[2]

Now, the question is: could one see an analogous meaning in Psyche's gesture? From this point of view, if darkness stays in short for the micro-absences of the object necessary for the development of the capacity to symbolize, the lighting of the lamp would not be a *real* transgression but would testify to awareness of the ineluctability of the end of life. But, from another angle, the first one forewarns the second, and it would be nothing more than a double figure of the negative, one put inside the other. It goes without saying that the need to endure a certain darkness could be read not only as a foreshadowing of the inevitability of the end of life but also of a certain denial of it and, therefore, of the need for the lie. Finally, in a speculative key, it would also reflect the dark background of sense; the pre-categorical and unthematizable dimension of being from which the entity that is the subject rises and the mystery of the love impulse generates (Cupid is always depicted as blindfolded).

As we can see, therefore, to intuit that the essence of a relationship is what matters, as Green (1993) says, is to understand the work of the negative. Language is *par excellence* the place of the negative, in the sense that since we have names for things, we are never again in the absolute presence or absolute absence of the object.

The cure

I'll present now a clinical fragments that resonate with the concept of aesthetic conflict and illustrate how the theoretical discourse carried out so far can "translate" into a technique and find practical application in the clinic.

Mr Noone

[The following is the text of another clinical supervision session.]

The colleague reads an English text of an exchange with her patient that occurred in another language. The patient is complaining that no one sees him:

> P. *Yes, I needed to be number one . . . like the apple of one's eye. It is a very sad thing that a person does not have any idea, any preconception of one's own . . . very weird and pathetic. . . . As if I am nothing. . . . A. What do you mean?*
> P. *I am thinking about the past. . . . I am such a person who noone wants to know, to talk to, who doesn't have an idea about anything . . . I wonder if I am still like that . . . insufficient, incapable, and ugly . . . like a rock bar toilet, everywhere is black.*

While I listen and scroll the text with my eyes, I'm surprised when I read the "*noone*" – written like this, without a break – and like in a musical score preceded by three notes of "one" (TA-TA-TA-PUM!). I can't help but read a big NO, because in Italian the suffix "-one" works as an augmentative, expressing more intensity. So, I can host the wild idea that unconsciously and with the contribution of two successive translations and the new field of supervision, the patient can express unconsciously and with much greater effectiveness the insurmountable wall behind which he feels locked up: the enormous NO that others oppose him, and that, of course, we can think from different points of view: historical, intrapsychic, relational and intersubjective (field). The absent object (the "no one") becomes a present but intensely persecutory object that says NO to the patient's request for existence.

I realize that this example can make you smile, but I limit myself to an infinitesimal fragment, for lack of space, and because, in essence, the method is the same even if the scale of magnitude varies. The "noone", which has become a NO ONE!!! (in Italian we sometimes say with emphasis and dragging the first syllable – *noo'*-NE! – to reiterate with a certain impatience and boredom a "no" already given to someone who does not seem to want to accept it), turns into a character-function of the field of which, from now on, we must have the utmost consideration.

For me, surprise is the sign of an intuition that is not only rational but also affective, playful, poetic, bodily, integrated and somato-psychic. That's why it tastes true. If the reaction is shared, between supervisor and supervisee, a little bit of truth is created that brings some order to a situation of disorder, a micro-experience of creating sense and meaning, a happy musical moment, a little brick that expands the mind, a new idea (hopefully with a nice Apgar score) – literally, a memorable episode. It will then be a matter during the supervision session and then again when the analyst returns to the sessions with the patient to see what this character or emotional function of the field does or does not do, where it comes from, how it relates to other characters, etc.

It is also an example of a micro-transformation into hallucinosis, because at the origin, there is only a tiny mistake in typing the text. As in the case of Russian dolls, placed one inside the other, the most internal one would be to consider NOONE, not only from the point of view of the history or intrapsychic constitution of the patient or of the character-hologram of the field of analysis, but also of the hypothetical character of the field of supervision. For me, the method of psychoanalysis has its own intrinsic beauty because it allows us to find a red thread in this complexity (which is the complexity of the human) without simplifying it, reducing it to something else, or eliminating it.

On the technical level, thinking in terms of the dream of the session – or of the characters of the fiction of the analysis – does not mean in any way to make all this explicit to the patient, but simply to add to the tools we already have (conscious identification, rational understanding, empathy, etc.) an even more sophisticated compass. This is one of the essential points in the paradigm shift that took place after Bion and with the centrality of the intersubjective moment in the creation of the mind.

The mother-child relationship and intercorporeity

Having a convincing model of the development of the child in the relationship with the mother is essential to grasp the importance in analysis not
only of semiotic communication and of the *aesthetic* and *intersubjective*
constitution of the subject, but also of how one can never ignore a basic
conceptual (linguistic) matrix. There is no thought without concepts. But
then we should be more aware of the fact that the relationship between
minds is not only "mental" or abstract, but also musical, aesthetic, corporeal, and that the body that concerns psychoanalysis is not the anatomical
body but the lived body, not "the inanimate" of science but the world of
life. It means updating the concept of the repressed unconscious with that
of a non-repressed unconscious – an unconscious not made up of representations but which is not, for this reason, totally outside of language, not
outside of the laws that are deposited in it, and, therefore, in the end, not
totally outside of the repressed – or, strictly speaking, not an un-repressed
unconscious but a non-representational unconscious. One can, therefore,
maintain the idea, inherent in the concept of repression, of something split,
not integrated, not transformed, and which is a source of psychological
suffering, even if not so much in the hyper-specific sense of a single pathogenic representation, but as a misalignment with respect to the "interpretations" that sociality gives of each individual by defining their identity. In
essence, the repressed pathogenic content would testify to a failure of the
subject's alpha function. It would be an agglomeration of emotions that the
psyche has not been able to transform in order to give meaning to experience – no longer a foreign body of the psyche, but a stretch mark or a hole
of meaning.

What can we derive from this point of view for treatment?

If in the first case – that of representational intentionality – we can always
aspire to a type of knowledge with clear and circumscribed contents (or
at least presume them, if unconscious), then in the second case – that of
bodily intentionality – we can only aspire to a more or *less* blurred knowledge. And what would that be? Knowledge represented by the feeling of
"keeping time" in the process of mutual recognition described earlier, like
passing from a stiff motility to a loose and light gait: something one "feels"

but would not be able to explain in words clearly, just as it is impossible to translate music. A good playing together [*suonare*] or a "re-sonating" [*ri-suonare*].

With respect to this kind of dance or jazz session of being in a relationship of minds, emotions can be reliable indicators. We can consider emotions as indicators or clues of the vicissitudes of *praktognosia* – the procedural knowledge of a couple or field in a given moment. On the one hand, emotions are part of this music of the body, and on the other hand, as in the case of music, they admit a certain *indirect* translatability in precise notations. Music is an asemantic language but not an asymbolic one. Just as the living sensation I receive from listening to an adage can be transcribed on a musical score in notes and pauses, without giving me back anything *directly* of the sensorial experience, so can I order the emotions I feel under Bion's letters of H, L, K. From Merleau-Ponty (1945/2002), we could borrow the metaphor of the *atmosphere* and qualify it as emotional to indicate what the inattentive attention of the analyst is directed toward.

The approach of classical psychoanalysis is aimed at deconstructing the discourse in order to discover the clues of forbidden representations, the fruit of an intentionality of action limited to the subjectivity of the patient – that is to say, to the ego seen in an atomistic sense, and responsible for the *de-formations* of the patient's judgements and behaviours. Although upside down, it is still the Descartes ego that we are dealing with. That Bion's ego is not a re-edition of Cartesian dualism is demonstrated by the fact that he instead puts emotion back at the centre of psychoanalysis, where Freud positions representation. But he understands emotion as the elementary human form, inevitably corporeal and transindividual, distilling a first sense for the lived experience starting from that of the mouth-breast encounter. In my opinion, this is his anti-dualistic and anti-psychologistic vision that is not restricted to the perspective of the isolated subject, and clearly expressed in the true intersubjective concept of the "protomental system". This is not a dimension taken away from the human area of the symbolic and of language, but instead a dimension that – I repeat – excludes neither sense nor meaning as we have defined them already.

In this model, there is no longer any subject/object dualism or psyche/body dualism. If anything, the Freudian assertion of the Ego as a corporeal Ego finds an effective theoretical realization – but so should the opposite: the body also should be seen as if it were, as always, an "egoic" body – that is, a body that is written by culture. The opacity of the presumed "mystical" attitude in Bion as a model of a psychoanalysis of corporeity is then justified by the opacity of what we define precisely as corporeal intentionality, whose sense, and not meaning, can only be approached *indirectly*. What does this intuiting the operating intentionality of the field consist of? In disposing oneself to a receptivity that is both passive and active. In the very act of grasping signals of how the (inter)corporeal (emotional) field generates, instant by instant and anonymously, the ineliminable background for the acts of lucid consciousness, *contributing to give them a form* or *to trans-form* life experience.

From this point of view, Freudian psychoanalysis still appears deeply rooted in a psychology of representation and that of Bion in a psychology of body's knowledge and of an emotional or intercorporeal relationality. The shift from one paradigm to another did not happen by chance. But, instead, it is justified by the relevant weight that, in the genesis of psychic suffering, has been attributed to the traumatic events of the phase in which the primary constitution of the psyche occurs, which can only be intersubjective and aesthetic. If that is where the damage occurred, we must have as precise a theory as possible of where and how to intervene. In my opinion, such a theory should include the idea that the meanings sedimented at the level of the body's functions are of a "procedural" or "implicit" or "non-representational" nature. They belong to a semiotic order, but, for this reason, not outside the area of what is human or of language – just the symbolic or, more precisely, the semantic side of it.

Notes

1 "Master of the Straus Madonna" is the pseudonym given to an unknown Italian artist who worked in Florence toward the beginning of the fifteenth century.
2 "Und als plötzlich jäh / der Gott sie anhielt und mit Schmerz im Ausruf / die Wrote sprach: Er hat sich umgewendet -, / begriff sie nights une sagte leise: Wer?".

References

Apuleius, L. (2006). *Cupid and Psyche*. London: Penguin. (Original work from *Metamorphoses*, also called *The Golden Ass*, written in the 2nd century AD).
Bion, W.R. (1970). *Attention and Interpretation: A Scientific Approach to Insight in Psycho-Analysis and Groups*. London: Tavistock.

Bion, W.R. (1977). The past presented. In: *A Memoir of the Future* (pp. 219–426). London: Karnac, 1991.

Calvino, I. (1952). *Our Ancestors: The Cloven Viscount, the Baron in the Trees, the Nonexistent Knight*. London: Vintage, 1998.

Fichte, J.G. (1794/1868). *Science of Knowledge*. Philadelphia: J. B. Lippincott & Co.

Gaddini, E. (1982). Early defensive fantasies and the psychoanalytical process. *International Journal of Psycho-Analysis*, 63:379–388.

Green, A. (1993). *The Work of the Negative*. London: Karnac.

Grotstein, J.S. (2004). The seventh servant: The implications of a truth drive in Bion's theory of 'O'. *International Journal of Psycho-Analysis*, 85:1081–1101.

Kristeva, J. (1982). *Powers of Horror: An Essay on Abjection*. New York: Columbia University Press. (Original work published 1980)

Lacan, J. (1966). *Écrits, First Complete Edition in English*. New York: W. W. Norton & Company, 2006. (Original work published 1966)

Meltzer, D. (1973). *The Apprehension of Beauty*. Strathtay, Scotland: Clunie Press.

Merleau-Ponty, M. (1945). *Phenomenology of Perception*. London: Routledge, 2002.

Nietzsche, F. (1995). *Thus Spoke Zarathustra: A Book for All and None*. New York: Modern Library.

Ogden, T.H. (1994). *Subjects of Analysis*. Lanham, MD: Jason Aronson.

Ovid. (2008). *Metamorphoses* (E.J. Kenney, Ed. & A.D. Melville, Trans.). Oxford: Oxford University Press. (Original work published 8 AD).

Pinkard, T. (1996). *Hegel's Phenomenology: The Sociality of Reason* (p. 9). Cambridge: Cambridge University Press.

Rilke, R.M. (1907). *Neue Gedichte*. Leipzig: Im Insel-Verlag.

Schilder, P.F. (1950). *The Image and Appearance of the Human Body*. London: Routledge.

Winnicott, D.W. (1949). Hate in the counter-transference. *The International Journal of Psychoanalysis*, 30:69–74.

Žižek, S. (1989). *The Sublime Object of Ideology*. New York: Verso, 2009.

Chapter VII

Going for a stroll

The root of emotions

The violence of expulsion

A patient named Carlo asks for a consultation because he is suffering from "premature ejaculation". He describes a turbulent love life that involves a succession of girlfriends who trigger in him a series of fits of jealousy and anger that sometimes end up with him physically abusing them.

The images that come to mind are of containers so crammed full of contents that they explode.

The plot seems to me to involve a container that is inadequate to contain overly intense emotions, which lead to the container itself exploding, accompanied by the violent dispersion of contents and consequent instances of acting out.

Carlo had always made his girlfriends sign a kind of contract promising not to abandon him.

"Terror of abandonment" seems to be the *triggering factor* for the whole situation.

He turns up for his second appointment twenty-five minutes early (!).

He then describes a party at which a colleague of his had flirted with his current girlfriend but he hadn't felt anything. He seems therefore to alternate between "no relationship" and "explosive relationship", or between "no intercourse" and "premature ejaculation".

Interpretation can be brought back to three different contexts

- In the first context, communications are gathered together inside a receptacle and then introduced in increasing quantities into the current

DOI: 10.4324/9781003279020-7

relationship, until they become the hypodermic needle of transference interpretations.

- In the second, communications are spread out across a field (in the Baranger sense of the term) which periodically collapses owing to the interpretation given to the bastion created by the gestalt made up of the blind spots of both patient and analyst – and then the cycle goes on.
- The third is the unsaturated field, the result of the various groupings made up of analyst and patient that are immersed in a dreamlike atmosphere where often "it evolves" only by virtue of the analyst's enzymatic interventions.

It evolves

This is a phrase used by Bion in one of his last seminars, in which he expressed his confidence that the field will by its very nature evolve as long as it is not too perturbed by the analyst's need to interpret. There are, however, some factors we can point to that are at work even when we are not aware of them.

The alpha function is constantly at work; it transforms sense data into pictograms and thus into waking dream thought, the building blocks for thinking.

Night dreams reorganize all the pictograms "constructed" during the day, sorting them out into narratives belonging to different possible genres and styles.

Transformations into dreams and transformations into play, the session as a dream and transformations into stories all operate within the session, de-concretizing, alphabetizing and de-constructing the inaccessible "O's".

The session can be viewed as a *dream that recounts itself* as it gradually unfolds in a sort of continuous reverie.

Group defences

The dominant culture and religion can be seen as shared and transmissible ways of managing primitive and barely containable emotions via a set of rules that modulates and contains them.

A girl whose emotional explosiveness is not easy to contain finds no better solution than to convert to Islam, which provides her with a battery of guarantees against the incontinence she fears. Closer to home (by which

I mean Italy), we can think of how the Catholic religion has constructed a whole system of checks and balances to regulate emotions, fears, anxieties and doubts.

Stefano and attention deficit

Stefano is brought in for consultation because he is suffering from attention deficit syndrome. What emerges clearly is that the atmosphere in which he lives (and his own psychic atmosphere) is characterized by small but frequent and incessant emotional "mini-tsunamis", whirlwinds of anger, jealousy and dread of abandonment. Periodically he unleashes bursts of profanity that are reminiscent of Tourette's syndrome.

We might picture the chart of his emotions as being continually punctuated by tsunamis.

The same session will feature both a "pterodactyl scream" and a robot hiss, with oscillations between them.

The path that will lead Stefano away from his dinosaur evacuations and digitized world of robots will be a long one.

What will make this happen is the passage from a digitized yes-no-yes to a "yes but"/"no but" world in which cushioning the "no" or limiting the "yes" will enable the discovery of a "human code" starting from the evacuation by the pterodactyl in the form of scribbles, stains and tangles or the robot's yes/no.

Factors of recovery

I believe that what we say makes up 30 per cent of these factors, how we say it 25 per cent and the remaining 45 per cent consists of what we do mentally – mostly without knowing it – in our sessions with the patient. It is, therefore, the so-called non-specific factors that dominate. We label them thus to cover up our ignorance, to celebrate the known and thus steer clear of the paths of the unknown. Actually, though, this is what should be our privileged terrain of research.

Historical memory and what lies beneath

Nicola remembers that as a child he was always afraid his mother would forget to come and pick him up from school and he would be abandoned.

But beneath this scene, and crucially defining it, are many other and different scenes: there is the repeated experience of minds (his mother's mind or that of other caregivers) that were unavailable, or for the most part unavailable; or occluded, or for the most part occluded.

Upstream from this lies the game of projective identifications or beta evacuations and their destiny.

One possible metaphor for this is the mobile phone and the charger (where roles are reversed): we know very little about the pathology of the "charger".

If the mind is occluded or unavailable, the beta elements are not only not transformed but are charged with heightened intensity.

Obviously, there is a whole range of possible intermediate situations between the success and failure of alphabetization, including that of the unpredictable object that drives a person mad. But there is also the state of "trompe-l'oeil availability" in which "Ah, really?" was the unfailing response of a mother who had never understood her son's explicit or implicit requests.

Phobias

When faced with a phobia, we can consult our manual and find confirmation of what we already know, or we can depart from the known terrain of our "basic-level encyclopaedia" and open our minds up to the fantasies sparked off by the given situation.

If someone has a phobia of lifts or of confined spaces, in addition to the whole range of the other known fears – fear of collapse, fear of dependence, fear of trusting others – one could also think of the lift as having room for Mario, say, but not for the Mario's split-off "gorilla", which finds itself stuck in a *claustrum*, a structure that is too rigid and too small compared to the goods lift he would need. And what do we do with this gorilla? Why and how did it come to mind? Do these split-off functionings lack oxygen if placed inside the lift cage? Or are they functionings that have been sent into orbit with the phobia bearing the only residual imprint?

The idea of someone with a phobia of knives inevitably calls to mind *Secrets of a Soul*, the film directed by Georg Wilhelm Pabst, where the main character, Martin Fellmann, develops precisely this symptom. The result is that he ends up being spoon fed by his mother after learning that his young and attractive male cousin is coming to visit and that his beautiful young wife is very intrigued by this news. So, is jealousy at play here? Or is it rather a case of fear of the most passionate side of his nature ("the cousin"), whose arrival on the scene he has difficulty putting up with, and which he would like to eliminate because it is too intense? What story will it be possible to construct starting from the narreme "fear of knives"?

If someone has a phobia of their own emotions, which are so wild as to be terrifying, what could very well develop is a phobia of emotional truths that leads him to take refuge in lies. The liar is constantly caught in the crossfire between the Superego and the emotions that might be triggered by emotional contact. The liar's strategy is to deconstruct the facts and to come up with a lie that replaces them. Essentially the lie is an excess of clothes to cover the naked truth, clothes whose function is not to make the truth bearable but to conceal it more than is necessary. The lie stands in relation to transformations into hallucinosis as truth does to transformations into dreams.

If someone has a phobia of their emotions and alternates bulimic and anorexic behaviour, and this same person tells us about their fear of being bitten by their neighbour's dogs, one way of addressing the situation is to take a look at the paths that might be taken by these emotions that bite and rip apart, and that are either put to sleep by consuming loads of food or debilitated by the lack of nourishment.

If someone has a phobia of death and insists on talking about jealousy (the Italian word "gelosia" contains the element "gelo", meaning cold), one might see the fear of the cold as a fear of death and regard the whirlwind of emotions he is overwhelmed by and trapped inside as the most effective antifreeze (in Italian, "antigelo") available to him on the shelves of his mind.

To borrow once again the words of Ogden, phobias speak clearly to us of clumps of the mind that we have been unable to dream and thus integrate into our emotional DNA.

Of course, this list could go on indefinitely, taking in, for example, phobia of dirt and fear of animals. However, there is one phobia that all analysts share, and that is the phobia of the unknown, which often makes us cling to what we already know rather than venture to explore uncharted territory.

Potential identities

These are all identities or functionings that usually remain silent in deactivated modes of aggregation, but which become activated and available, or come into play in particular and unusual circumstances.

We find these identities where the double is a part or mode of functioning that is split-off and alternative to our way of being (Dr Jekyll and Mr Hyde are a case in point).

As with a murderous mode of functioning, where we need to activate a sort of "death constellation" that corresponds to certain precise points in our mental life (such as selecting numbers for the combination on a safe), so other constellations can be activated even completely out of the blue. We might speak for example of a constellation of cowardice (Don Abbondio), one of heroism (Pietro Micca), and one of falling in love (Anna Karenina).

Of course, there is a potentially infinite number of identities that, normally in sleep, can be activated under different conditions.

At times some of these identities (or modes of functioning) are active within us without our knowledge, and must be deactivated to allow proper mental functioning to be resumed.

There are times when some of these identities cannot be put to sleep and, if they are not first repaired, continue to create a disturbance.

The cow on the raft

I am thinking, for example, of Carlotta, a brilliant university lecturer who is tormented, without her knowledge, by a constellation that could be called the Nativity Scene with Baby Jesus. The nativity scene had been swept away by floods leaving only fragments behind, like a cow drifting on a raft. Until it was dreamt of, this "catastrophe" took the form of a compulsive need to forcibly take care of people in great pain; here it was the "child in need of primary care" identity that needed to come into being and to be recognized.

Abandonment

Arguably, this is a question that is over-interpreted by some analysts – at every weekend or at every separation.

In my view this is something that must be understood within the specific context of each individual's psychic life.

There are certain shared narratives that can sometimes be usefully deployed, such as the fairy tale of the Little Match Girl or the story of Jason and Medea. But then the specific nature of this mental experience must be understood in terms of each individual's psychic life.

There is a "ground zero" of abandonment that must also be identified, together with the points $0.1 \rightarrow 0.2 \rightarrow 0.3$, which represent transformations that are often developmental. For example, abandonment can be expressed in the image of an elderly man who depends on caregivers to change his continence pad and keep him alive. But it could also be the "ground zero" moment of a very young child. At this point distracted "carers" appear who do not meet the child's needs and an autistic nucleus is formed as a defence against emotional overflow.

A patient connects her anguish at being abandoned with an image from her stock of memories: the image of "a drowning cow" when a river in Veneto overflowed. This almost seems to be a pictogram of abandonment: the raft for the cow is an idea that could readily be developed.

Abandonment and depression are firmly bound together by the memory of the depressed father who exorcised his depression through games that became gradually ever more "extreme" and risky.

Carlo and hidden identities

Carlo is a highly regarded professional who asks for an analysis because he deals with anger by at first saying nothing but then getting absolutely incensed and flying off the handle. Other details make it immediately clear that he suffers from continuous and sudden oscillations between incontinence and hypercontinence.

The only antidote to losing his temper seems to be locking himself up inside "a cage of rules" – the obsessive rituals that accompany him throughout the day. A successful man, he rapidly introduces other characters such as "a brother who stutters and is one of life's losers, a wife who is extremely anxious and in need of care, and a brother-in-law suffering from a severe form of diabetes who has attempted suicide on several occasions".

It seems to me that we can create a scene that involves all of these characters. The question will be whether it is possible to "waterproof" Stefano against his other identities or whether these will have to be "treated" separately before they can be better integrated.

Fragility, dependence, despair, misfortune – how can these be transformed so that Stefano will be able to accept them as his own?

Panic attacks

Of course, there are numerous possible types of "attack": attacks of anger, attacks of jealousy, attacks of migraine, which all imply that the emotion involved can be recognized as anger, jealousy, etc.

Panic attacks, on the other hand, seem to be less specific than others and to be marked by an implicit accentuation of the explosive aspect: in other words, the exploding emotions are less worked through. It is as if panic were more closely connected to characteristic "explosiveness" and as if what exploded were emotional states as yet insufficiently elaborated.

Narrative Big Bang

The Big Bang is set off at every analytic encounter and brings into being unpredictable universes that force us to go where the patient wants us to go (in analytic jargon, to be in unison): the obsessional Arts Faculty librarian; the bedside of a dying aunt; the boat show with the two horrible employers.

Only if the patient feels comfortable enough in the story – both in himself or herself and within the analytic pair – can the patient move forward smoothly. Expressed in jargon, this would mean: experiencing a degree of unison that makes analytic dialogue comfortable.

In some models this is where the interpretative caesura should come to life, which can manifest itself in many different ways.

Doctor and acrobat

Is psychoanalysis a profession? My view of "psychoanalysts" is minimalist: in my opinion, they have particular and specific skills only when it comes to the treatment of psychic suffering.

For there to be a psychoanalyst there must also be a patient and a setting; outside this triad there is no such thing as a "psychoanalyst".

In my opinion, psychoanalysis is a "potion" that draws on science, craftsmanship, art and orthodoxy in varying parts.

In work the analyst uses all these elements to varying degrees.

It is my firm belief that among the many shifting identities that mark out psychoanalysts, they are above all "magicians". They perform magic with sounds, images and words; they exorcise demons; they ride dragons and so on. In other words, they throw open the space of fantasy, imagination, the absurd, the terrifying. He is a Jules Verne, a Fellini, a Bergman, a Brecht.

The point to emphasize, though, is that the psychoanalyst is always a "co-author" and never *the* author. These productions are "fleeting"; no one if not the two co-authors will know anything about the ephemeral worlds that have been opened up and closed down. The psychoanalyst is a magician by virtue of transforming what happens into dreams and into play; and a magician because of the opening up of *mise en abyme* scenarios.

For example:

- 10.30 am: the psychoanalyst is in a wooden tree house that is part of a famous hotel in Vermont, where the wedding night of an alternative young couple (but "alternative" to what?) is consummated;
- 11.30 am: the psychoanalyst goes back and forth between an operating theatre where a surgeon "removes blackberries whose tasty juice stops children from crying" and the mid-life crisis the same patient is going through;
- 12.30 pm: the psychoanalyst is with Ivan Ilyich, the protagonist of a story of pain and illness;
- 1.30 pm: the psychoanalyst is in the desert, abandoned, alone, worried: the patient does not come to the first session after the summer holidays (what goes around comes around);
- 2.30 pm: the psychoanalyst is a woman candidate in analysis who discovers her depression and whose femininity blossoms;
- 3.30 pm: the psychoanalyst is a violent borderline case, appearing in a film with Humphrey Bogart;
- 4.30 pm: the psychoanalyst is in a supervision teaching everything the psychoanalyst hasn't done for years but which must also be learnt;
- 5.30 pm: another supervision with an expert colleague; the psychoanalyst opens up to new textures; do saturated and stereotypical characters exist?
- 6.30 pm: the psychoanalyst is with a child with "Asperger's" who encounters first emotions . . .
- 7.30 pm: on the way home the analyst dissolves . . . and Dr Ferro goes out to dinner . . . or in the evening, worn out, the psychoanalyst often finds consolation on the home "couch", being brain washed by *Profiling* or *Homeland*, interrupted several times by phone calls, most of

them stupid, which the psychoanalyst has learned to cope with easily; then the psychoanalyst reads today's paper and, courtesy of the Internet, tomorrow's too.

This is the psychoanalyst's way of being able to come back on stage the following day even when not knowing what costume to wear, putting on a show that is part *Tonight We Improvise* and part *Two Authors in Search of Characters*. The psychoanalyst will be an actor, a poet, a writer, a companion, a dog, a tent or whatever else is required. Less and less, though, will the psychoanalyst be Sherlock Holmes, or Pasteur, and more and more Shakespeare; the psychoanalyst may also find himself or herself transformed into Diderot and coming up with the words: "Make yourself at home, Emma!" (the mistake is deliberate because history is always new!).

Chapter VIII

Towards an ethics of responsibility

Notes in the margins of Bion/ Rickman correspondence[1]

Tankishness

"It won't be complete Ritz-like luxury but it will be better than Russia." So writes Bion, with affectionate irony, of his new home in his last letter to Rickman (his 27th).

But, thinking about it, it's always the same with Bion. Whether it be in books, seminars (from the portrait that emerges in the accounts of those who participated), or in the consulting room (based on the impression we are able to get from vignettes recounted mostly in *Second thoughts* [Bion, 1967]), nothing is ever "Ritz-like luxury". There is always a kind of "tankishness" (Souter, 2009), a certain coarseness, in both the character of the man and the thought he expresses. He acknowledges it, too. In *Cogitations* (1992) he writes of his own difficulty in maintaining the ability to think clearly when faced with pressing violent emotions such as irritation and anger, even in everyday situations.

The soldier also emerges in his letters to Rickman, primarily because Bion was permanently scarred by his experience as a member of a tank crew in World War I and by the tragedies he witnessed; then because the war and the postwar period form the social backdrop of his analysis with Rickman and their collaboration in the selection of officers at the War Office Selection Board and at Northfield Hospital (from 1942 to 1943). Indeed, the letters extend over a lengthy period of time from 1939 to 1951.

A certain dry, militaristic tone is also sometimes perceptible in Bion's essay writing. The pounding rhythm with which the verbs "must" and "obey" resound when he emphasizes that the things which matter in the session are the unknown and what is happening in the present (see later); when he warns that the search for the truth must be pursued without compromise; when he argues that analyst and patient are like two wild and

DOI: 10.4324/9781003279020-8

frightened animals in the consulting room; when he explains that thought itself is an arduous and fragile conquest.

Yet he is a strange kind of soldier: on the one hand he appreciates discipline, which he continually exhorts analysts to adopt in their work, whereas on the other hand, as Hinshelwood writes, he has an "irascible impatience with authority" (2000, p. 8). His antipathy to the narrowness of mind, if not the typical stupidity, of military environments could be one of the reasons that led him to adopt a position that was disconcerting but successful. Whether as theorist, analyst or supervisor, Bion always assumes responsibility of command in the same original and paradoxical way: by renouncing it. He demonstrates leadership by (apparently) evading the role of leader. For him, the important thing is not so much to tell others what they must do, but to enable them to learn from experience, and thereby develop their own capacity to think and their own sense of responsibility.

It is this essential element, in both his character and his technique, which is the first feature that Bion seems to have taken from Rickman (or in any case shares with him), as we shall see.

Rickman as psychoanalytic mentor and mentor to Bion

In addition, covering the letters received from Bion, Conci (2011, this issue) offers the reader a useful summary of Rickman's scientific work. We learn that Rickman also has a marked antidogmatic attitude and an aversion to uncompromising rigidity in the exercise of power as an end in itself. As an author, Rickman respects the reader, presenting his ideas in an open way rather than dropping them from on high, offering only something that *could* be taken into consideration. We might say that both are reluctant soldiers (Bion claims that enlisting was the worst thing he ever did). Perhaps that is why their joint venture at Northfield ended so rapidly. It went on for six weeks but then failed because their unconventional methods clashed with the conservatism of the establishment.

Yet for Rickman, antidogmatism is not only an ethical position, but also an epistemological position. This is evident in an essay about the speculative character of theory and the risks of prematurely saturating experience with prior knowledge, and on the specific problems of psychoanalysis as a scientific discipline. These themes are also destined to form the backbone of Bion's thought.

The conception of epistemology that Rickman puts forward in his essay "Scientific Method and Psychoanalysis" (1945/2003) anticipates that of Bion. The title itself is echoed in the extraordinary *Attention and Interpretation*, published by Bion in 1970, which is subtitled *A Scientific Approach to Insight in Psycho-analysis and Groups*. Rickman also clearly addresses the problem of the *many* psychoanalytic models in "Number and the Human Sciences" in 1951 (Rickman, 1951). One might speculate that it is here that Bion's impulse to construct a metatheory, rather than add yet another theory to the existing ones, originates. In his view, only a theory of the common elements of psychoanalysis, the concepts gathered in the Grid, would be able to reconcile the opposing factions that emerged from the controversial discussions between the followers of Klein and those of Anna Freud between 1941 and 1942.

The typical air of abstraction found in Bion's concepts of function, faith, O, alpha and beta elements, and so on is derived from this preoccupation. These concepts are like those abstract paintings one might see in modern and contemporary art galleries that the author has called *Untitled*. The intention is to give them as much life as possible, beyond their ideological fences and the barriers represented by the reification of concepts. Bion intends to bring to psychoanalysis a higher level of formalization and to give it a more secure scientific basis; at the same time, however, he proposes to use psychoanalysis to understand scientific epistemology in general. It is clear that the realization of the project has gone far beyond the initial intention, as far as to produce a new – and, for some, shocking – paradigm in psychoanalysis.

The same epistemological sensitivity, which Freud also notably demonstrates, can be found in the emphasis that Rickman places on the significance of the experience shared by the patient and the analyst. For Rickman also, psychoanalysis is based on an experience of the present; it "operates in an *a-historical present*". The facts upon which the analyst draws to validate his hypothesis are generated in the here-and-now of the session. This is made very clear in "Experimental Psychology and Psychoanalysis", an essay written between 1937 and 1939 (Rickman, 1939), which is exactly the same period during which Bion is in analysis with Rickman. The coincidence is significant in view of the central role that the theme assumes in Bion's thinking. Facts that cannot be directly observed in the session, history, theories, preconceived hierarchies of meaning, are in themselves irrelevant or secondary. Mostly, they are obstacles.

Bion is particularly clear on this – there can be no misunderstanding. He puts his uniform back on. It is worth considering a fairly lengthy extract from an article first published in 1967 in *Psychoanalytic Forum*, to hear the categorical tone with which the soldier Bion is at the service of the "pseudo-mystical" Bion and explains, in an assertive style, the rules of psychoanalytic observation:

> Psychoanalytic "observation" is concerned neither with what has happened nor with what is going to happen, but with what is happening. Furthermore, it is not concerned with sense impressions or objects of sense. . . . Every session attended by the psychoanalyst *must* have no history and no future. . . . What is "known" about the patient is of no further consequence: it is either false or irrelevant. . . . The only point of importance in any session is the unknown. Nothing *must* be allowed to distract from intuiting that. . . . *Obey the following rules*. . . . *Do not* remember past sessions . . . *no* crisis should be allowed to breach this rule. . . . The psychoanalyst can start by avoiding any desires for the approaching end of the session (or week, or term). Desires for results, 'cure' or even understanding *must not* be allowed to proliferate. . . . These *rules must be obeyed* all the time and not simply during the session. . . . If this *discipline* is followed, there will be an increase of anxiety in the psychoanalyst at first, but it *must not* interfere with preservation of the rules. The procedure *should* be started at once and not be abandoned on any pretext whatever.
>
> (Bion, 1992, pp. 380–382, emphasis added)

The increase of anxiety occurs "because there is no barrier against fears of acknowledged dangers. . . . No barrier against guilt because of no known substitute for acknowledged and conventional therapeutic aims . . . [there is] isolation from group basic assumptions" (Bion, 1992, p. 296). The essential thing is not to inhibit the evolution of the session, the evolution or emergence of "O".

The reverie is the emotional truth that emanates directly from O, when O is allowed to evolve, and is also confirmation of reaching a first level of consensuality. It should be noted that Bion intends "to evolve", a term that might seem a concession to a vague mysticism, to mean something precise; yet the only place where he explains it is in the pages of *Cogitations*, which, as chance would have it, was a text not destined for publication. Bion writes that the analyst must simply give himself or herself the time to be passively visited, as in dream, by reveries (ideas or figurative impressions) (Bion, 1992), which offer an opportunity to grasp the meaning of what is happening at the level of unconscious communication *between* analyst and patient, that is, the emotional reality of the analytic field.

In this context, then, the evolution of O is nothing more than the way in which Bion names the "dream-like memory", the memory of psychic reality "the stuff of analysis" (1970, p. 70), in order to distinguish it from intentional and conscious memory that is based on sensory impressions. Yet Bion always prefers open definitions – at the edge of obscurity; in effect they are non-definitions – so as to push for the use of one's own head, to think one's own previously unthought thoughts. He seeks to be intentionally ambiguous. But he is not a mystic. He is Cartesian. He merely uses the language and the experience of the mystics as a means of expressing systematic doubt.

Evidence of Rickman's influence on Bion is also apparent in the essay "First Aid in Psychotherapy" (1936–1938). The patient's history, he states, is equivalent to the manifest content of dreams. The idea anticipates the concept of waking dream thought (absolutely central in Bion) and paves the way for the radical antirealism with which the session can be viewed, at least from the vertex of actual unconscious communication, in the theory of the analytic field (Civitarese, 2008; Ferro & Basile, 2009).

One could go on and on with the list of correspondences between the topics addressed by Rickman and bequeathed to Bion through a comparison of their respective scientific contributions. For example, the concept of "nameless dread" is adumbrated in an article by Rickman published in *The Lancet* in 1938 titled "Panic and Anxiety Reactions in Groups during Air Raids" (our thoughts turn to the extraordinary paintings by Henry Moore of London's refugees as almost dead souls in the tunnels of the underground, recently exhibited at the Tate gallery), where Rickman uses the expression "nameless horror" and sees it as the rekindling of an experience already lived in a stage in which the mind was still immature. The idea of the individual as a "field of forces" and of an ego constituted of an "internal society", in "The Influence of the 'Social Field' on Behavior in the Interview Situation" (1943), and the direct reference to the work of Kurt Lewin, are also worth mentioning.

The essential thing to understand about Bion's thought – which also involves *not* understanding it – is to realize the close parallel that exists between the theory of thought development, the conception of interpretation and of clinical work, and the vision of the dialectic that is established between the various psychoanalytic theories (and more generally of the way that scientific knowledge proceeds). The basic inspiration with which Bion drafts these various themes is absolutely uniform and consistent. In all cases, what counts are the transformations by which we move from emotionally chaotic and persecutory situations towards concepts or *abstractions* (the officer in battle does not have a different task).

The same interweaving between these different levels can be found earlier in Rickman's scientific production. Clinical theory, epistemology, scepticism, antiauthoritarianism, the intersubjective conception of the subject, and the concept of field are nodes of a conceptual network that he had already delineated remarkably coherently, as is clear, for example, from this passage taken from "Scientific Method and Psychoanalysis":

> The receptive tolerance that we extend to our patients is precisely the attitude which, alone, is genuinely favourable to free and constructive discussion. In fact, we seem to leave behind in the consulting room the attitude which is so urgently required in the theoretical research.
>
> (Conci, 2011, p. 7)

It is easy to infer from lines like this that Bion remains faithful to Rickman and continues to expand upon his theories. Of course, he adds his own genius. Let us now look at the letters.

The letters

If we turn to the letters, these first impressions are confirmed. It would be surprising, after all, if something different had happened. I will confine myself here to some rhapsodic observations.

In the 11th letter, the longest of all, we find again the themes of antidogmatism and the love for truth, the latter being another of the concepts central to (and also the most misunderstood in) Bion's thought, to the point that it is regarded as a real drive.

When Bion reflects on the issue of the selection of the officers, the global approach to confronting problems is evident: it is in fact a group approach. The democratic system of voting for possible candidates for the role of officer is equivalent to the idea of the patient as the best colleague. The soldiers *know* who is best suited to lead them. Similarly, the patient *knows* what happens from moment to moment, and could share unconscious knowledge of the state of receptiveness of the analyst if only the patient could be heard. The method devised by Bion and Rickman transforms the group from a basic assumption group to a work group. In the same way, the analyst has the task of helping the patient to move away from fragmentation and towards integration. Equally, the capacity for leadership grows if you give people experiences from which they are able to learn. The capacity to assume responsibility for life and to give personal meaning to existence increases through analysis, if it allows the patient to experience O. The best aspiring officers are those who know how to feel compassion for their comrades. The candidates for the role of officers of the psychic life are the thoughts without a thinker that need time to emerge – or what Bion calls stray thoughts.

This is clearly expressed in Bion's 24th letter (which dates 1946):

> I find that one important thing with patients – dreadfully important + I kick myself for not having seen it before – is the need to let them make their own experiments + approaches however hard and sterile they may appear to be. This time they need to feel in a family in which their [?] curiosity and intelligence is *not* turned off".
>
> (Conci, 2011, p. 84)

The experiment at Northfield (pertinently described by Hinshelwood as "perhaps the first and prototype reflective institution") (2000, p. 8) and the experience of selecting officers were crucial in directing Bion's thought. It is here that Bion's radical intersubjectivity and his theory of the social nature of the subject originates. When in 1943 the article "Intra-group Tensions in Therapy – Their Study as the Task of the Group" was published in *The Lancet* (Bion & Rickman, 1943) (an article that was to form the future first chapter of *Experiences in Groups and Other Papers* [Bion, 1961]), it aroused the enthusiasm of a French analyst little known at the time – Jacques Lacan. He went to London with the specific purpose of meeting the authors. He then wrote in an article:

> I find in their work something of the miraculous feeling of the initial stages of the Freudian elaboration: that of finding in the very impasse of a situation the vital force of an intervention . . . [the article] will mark a historic date in psychiatry.
>
> (1947, p. 15)

Besides this, he adds that he felt that he had the impression, he explains, that they were "pregnant with a birth of sorts that is a new outlook opening upon the world" (*ibid.*, 19), and creates a portrait of the two extraordinary personalities he had encountered:

> Thus, I am going to try to present these two men for you *au naturel*, men of whom it can be said that the flame of creation burns in them. In the first [Bion], this flame is as if frozen in a motionless and lunar mask accentuated by the thin commas of a black moustache . . . one of those beings who remain solitary even in the utmost commitment. . . . In the other [Rickman], this flame scintillates behind a lorgnette to the rhythm of a verb burning to return to action . . . with a smile which makes his fawn brush bristle.
>
> (*ibid.*, 15)

The precious material that Conci discovered in the archives of the British Psychoanalytical Society now happily completes Lacan's vivid and admirable description.

The 20th letter concerns the nature of society. The individual is merely a social animal who feels alone, weak and insecure. The individual needs a group to overcome fears. However, having grown stronger thanks to the group, the individual no longer tolerates anything that reminds him or her of this basic weakness. Specularly, the group favours the rise of its most ambitious and aggressive members. They give themselves to politics and reach positions of command. But this is not enough. They feel compelled to dominate their peers. Nations end up being governed by their more combative members. This is how Bion portrays authority, people who do not want to know anything about the tensions that pervade the group. Except that, in the end, the group itself is induced by its own suffering, for example by wars, to investigate the insecurity that it comes across, as the individual is by anxieties. But many obstacles impede the discovery of the insignificance and impotence of society as well as of the individual.

In this 20th letter, Bion gives an impressive description of the intimate nature of political power. In the foreground is the equation that the individual is equal to an internal group. Above all, it anticipates his reinterpretation of the Oedipus complex, in terms not of the sexual crime but of the desire/fear of knowledge. The persistent argument against institutions and the establishment, ridiculed in his late ("narrative") writings, results in an ethics of responsibility. Contradictions should be highlighted and negotiated, but without aiming for definitive solutions. But this is also the case in the analyst's consulting room.

The 21st letter confirms the connection between clinical theory and epistemology that I mentioned earlier. Speaking of group therapy, Bion stresses his interest in developing a theory of psychoanalytic observation and insists on the point that it is important to share data, experiences, hypotheses, that which evolves under the eyes of all the participants. Interpretations should concern not only an individual in the group but the "common factor", something that also has relevance for other members of the group. We see that, as Rickman had done, Bion emphasizes the present in the session in order to satisfy the requirements of the scientific method in psychoanalysis.

But speaking of the "common factor", I would say that if there is one element that may characterize the happy encounter between Bion and Rickman, it is the struggle against the common enemy of arrogant stupidity, of bigotry, of certainty and of mental narrowness. From the letters and the opportune synthesis of Rickman's scientific work, it is difficult to doubt the decisive influence these ideas exerted on Bion. As mentioned in the 13th letter, the baton that one passes to the other is the unconditional aspiration to nurture people of free spirit ("liberal minded people").

Note

1 Translated by Josie Gill.

References

Bion, W.R. (1961). *Experiences in Groups and Other Papers*. London: Tavistock.
Bion, W.R. (1967). *Second Thoughts. Selected Papers on Psychoanalysis*. London: Heinemann.

Bion, W.R. (1970). *Attention and Interpretation*. London: Karnac.

Bion, W.R. (1992). *Cogitations*. London: Karnac.

Bion, W.R., & Rickman, J. (1943). Intra-group tension in therapy – Their study as a task of the group. *The Lancet*, 242:678–681.

Civitarese, G. (2008). *The Intimate Room. Theory and Technique of the Analytic Field*. London: Routledge, 2010.

Conci, M. (2011). Bion and his first analyst, John Rickman (1891–1951): A revisitation of their relationship in the light of Rickman's personality and scientific production and of Bion's letters to him (1939–1951). *International Forum of Psychoanalysis*, 20:68–86.

Ferro, A., & Basile, R. (2009). *The Analytic Field: A Clinical Concept*. London: Karnac.

Hinshelwood, R.D. (2000). Foreword. In: T. Harrison (Ed.), *Bion, Rickman, Foulkes and the Northfield Experiments. Advancing on a Different Front* (pp. 7–10). London: Jessica Kingsley.

Lacan, J. (1947). British psychiatry and the war. *Psychoanalytical Notebooks of the London Circle*, 4:9–34.

Rickman, J. (1936). First aid in psychotherapy. In: P. King (Ed.), *No Ordinary Psychoanalyst. The Exceptional Contribution of John Rickman* (pp. 119–31). London: Karnac.

Rickman, J. (1939). Experimental psychology and psychoanalysis: A comparison of the techniques. In: P. King (Ed.), *No Ordinary Psychoanalyst. The Exceptional Contribution of John Rickman* (pp. 85–97). London: Karnac.

Rickman, J. (1943). The influence of the 'social field' on behaviour in the interview situation. In: P. King (Ed.), *No Ordinary Psychoanalyst. The Exceptional Contribution of John Rickman* (pp. 140–147). London: Karnac.

Rickman, J. (1945). Scientific method and psychoanalysis. In: P. King (Ed.), *No Ordinary Psychoanalyst. The Exceptional Contribution of John Rickman* (pp. 98–108). London: Karnac.

Rickman, J. (1951). Number and the human sciences. In: P. King (Ed.), *No Ordinary Psychoanalyst. The Exceptional Contribution of John Rickman* (pp. 109–118). London: Karnac.

Souter, K.M. (2009). The war memoirs: Some origins of the thought of W. R. Bion. *International Journal of Psychoanalysis*, 90:795–808.

Chapter IX

Freud's *Formulations on the Two Principles of Mental Functioning*

A possibly irreverent comment

There are different ways of approaching the models of the mind – one that I would like to call *continuist* and the other *discontinuist*. The former seeks to identify the common roots and analogies shared by concepts that emerged in different periods, while the latter emphasizes the existence of caesuras between the various models that make such a search superfluous.

What is the relationship between the concepts of Ego and alpha function?

Some might regard this as an interesting question; others may see it as irrelevant. When we read Freud's essay "Formulations on the Two Principles of Mental Functioning", we can only admire and be amazed by the brilliant way he constructs a coherent and functioning model of the mind.

The route he charts from the pleasure principle to the reality principle is extraordinary and, for those working within a Freudian model, the only possible path. Freud takes us by the hand to show us how the sick individual can be forced out of real life. It is the unbearable nature of real life that isolates the neurotic from it.

The neurotic always denies some fragment of reality.

Unconscious mental processes are the oldest; they are residues of a previous phase of development when the pleasure principle reigned supreme. Dreams can be seen as remnants of this mode of functioning.

Our psychic apparatus had to adapt to new needs partly in order to apprehend the sensory qualities of the outside world until such a time that there might be "impartial passing of judgement" as to the truth value or otherwise of a given idea.

At this point motor discharge is transformed into action, which in turn, by deferring discharge, turns into thinking.

Phantasying is a kind of no man's land. There is a delay in "educating the sexual instincts to pay regard to reality".

DOI: 10.4324/9781003279020-9

Freud also makes some fascinating remarks about religion, which shifts the pleasure principle into a future existence, and about education, which presses in the direction of the reality principle.

The choice of neurosis depends on the specific developmental phase the patient is going through at that moment.

The reality principle does not apply to unconscious processes.

Freud's construction is coherent and admirable, and for reasons of space my summary of it has been rather maladroit.

Nonetheless, in my opinion we still have to set it against the "catastrophic" events that have occurred over time vis-à-vis the central aspects of theory and technique in psychoanalysis.

Bion's different way of conceiving the unconscious

I would like to start from a metaphor used by Civitarese (2014) to help explain the concept of the unconscious in Freud. He compares it to a kind of maximum security prison, such as Alcatraz, where the sexual desires that were repressed during a child's developmental stages are locked up. Every now and then some inmates manage to escape from this maximum security prison, which is what produces dreams, slips, parapraxes, jokes, etc.

According to Freudian theory, therefore, the unconscious is formed primarily during the early stages of childhood, when the child must learn, through social rules, to give up the satisfaction of its sexual desires, which are then repressed and imprisoned in the unconscious. The prison guard of the unconscious – censorship – works in such a way as to ensure that when we dream, the contents of the unconscious are "disguised or masked" using the various mechanisms of dreaming: displacement, condensation, considerations of representability and secondary processing.

For Freud the unconscious is a source of drive energy that is crucial to the life of the individual but is also the source of many mental disorders. The task of psychoanalysis is thus to "unveil" the unconscious contents of our mind, to understand to what extent and in what way they influence our conscious life. With Bion the concept of the unconscious changes completely: it is formed continuously, both night and day, through the alpha function that constantly carries out the transformation of the beta elements – in other words, elements of pure sensoriality which as such cannot be thought – into alpha elements, pictograms that can then be used for dreams.

The transformation of beta elements into alpha elements leads to the formation of a sort of contact barrier, made up precisely of alpha elements, that produces a separation between conscious and unconscious. However, the alpha elements thus formed can be used by thought, and we find traces of them in the so-called narrative derivatives of waking dream thought. In other words, our mind is continuously engaged in this kind of process of digesting sense data that affect us both from the inside and from the out-side. Our mental health depends precisely on the digestive capacity of our mind, that is to say, on our ability to *create the unconscious*.

Working from this assumption, it is clear how the purpose of psycho-analysis has also changed since Bion – no longer the revelation of the unconscious, but the development of mental functions (above all the alpha function) to carry out the digestion/transformation of sensoriality into pic-tograms. The pictograms that form the unconscious can be used to create nocturnal dreams, but equally they are used during wakefulness for the narration of our experiences. For Bion, pathology and mental discomfort arise from a defective digestive capacity (the alpha function of the mind), or from a surfeit of beta elements – and thus of unthinkable sensoriality – which is then either projected towards the outside or causes discomfort in our body in the form of somatizations. Mental health, on the other hand, depends on our continuous ability to respond to sensory stimulation by creating visual images or dreaming about what happens to us also during the day. This is the so-called waking dream function.

Bion's different way of conceiving dreams

Dreams stop being the realm of the hallucinatory fulfilment of desire but serve in their two forms – diurnal (alpha function) and nocturnal (the dream properly understood as a "super alpha function"; Grotstein, 2007; Ferro, 2010) – to continually transform sensory data into pictograms, thought and narrations of reality.

However circumscribed it may be, "pathology", for example a symp-tom, speaks to us of defects in the mind's dream function in transforming that fact, that given fragment of reality, into a shareable, navigable and digestible narrative.

Examples abound: Professor Unrat in Heinrich Mann's eponymous novel was incapable of "dreaming" or "metabolizing" the finite nature of life, and indulged in massive doses of antidepressants (the dancer Lola Frohlich) to allay the "fact" that he could not come to terms with growing old.

The same goes for Carlotta, a patient who lives in a circular time frame that actually stops her from wearing a watch (both in a real and a metaphorical sense). When she finally begins to dream, and thus absorb, this "fact", she exclaims: "Here's my new watch". She then adds (jokingly but not that jokingly): "A gift from Father Christmas!".

Bion makes the point that someone should write a book titled *Interpretation of Reality*, in recognition of the function that dreams perform in all their different forms.

The different way of conceiving sexuality we owe to Bion

To Bion, sexuality is no longer to be seen as something that develops in phases, and as a discourse in the session we come to think of it not only as a drive but as a "narration" of the functioning of interacting minds – for example, of how projective identifications and reveries "mate" (Ferro, 2009).

If a male patient talks about his premature ejaculation, this will most likely refer to a lack of emotional control, explosive emotions that are narrated in a sexual narrative genre. The same goes for a woman patient who talks about vaginismus.

According to this model, one might think of a disproportion between insufficient containers and emotional hyper-contents – recounted through a sexual metaphor. This "sexual" tale could be replaced by any other narrative genre.

I am certainly no supporter of the hackneyed line: "Freud said it first!". And yet . . . and yet . . . and yet this short and densely argued paper contains the germs of many ideas that were later to be developed by others.

I refer in particular to the passage where Freud talks not only about the qualities of pleasure and unpleasure but also about the recognition by the conscious mind of sensory qualities.

In doing so, he paves the way for Bion's concept of the alpha function, which will come to be the great processor of sensoriality and whose significant attributes will be attention, notation and memory, alongside many others that remain unknown.

There is more. Also what Freud says about the passage from motor discharge → action → thought process opens the way for the mental apparatus to "tolerate an increased tension of stimulus while the process of discharge was postponed".

At this point we can see the conceptual building blocks being put together to form Bion's conceptualization of the concept of the container-contained.

Educating the drive, on the other hand, is something very different from containing, metabolizing and transforming it, as Bion (1997) reminds us in *Taming Wild Thoughts*.

I believe that the centrality of the sex drive has fallen away greatly, as has its associated development in phases as part of the evolution of the mind conceived as a specifically human characteristic. I am referring to that aspect of the mind that – starting from sensoriality and via containability, the alpha function and the nocturnal dream function – enables, in relations with others, the forging of the tools that go to make up the special quality of our minds. Nonetheless, evacuation will continue to be a defence mechanism, an unavoidable source of relationality and, in various forms, a necessary mode of alleviation for every individual mind, whether healthy or suffering.

Perhaps a few words need to be said about emotions and the necessary presence of emotions that will become central to the concepts of emotional pictograms.

I would like to conclude this part by talking about a short story by Chekhov titled "The Exclamation Mark". It is the story of a clerk whose job it is to write or copy files, a task he has performed meticulously for years. One day a colleague condescendingly accuses him of having little education, as evidenced by the fact that all he ever has to do is transcribe documents.

On returning home that night he finds himself unable to sleep because he keeps on going over in his mind all the documents – thousands, tens of thousands – he has written impeccably, and he remembers every possible rule about the use of commas, full stops, semicolons and even question marks.

Agitated and half-sleep, he stops in his tracks when his mind suddenly turns to exclamation marks. He doesn't remember ever having used one. When *are* they used?

He wakes up his wife. She is a highly educated woman who has completed all her college courses and who proudly tells him she knows all the rules of grammar by heart. She explains to him that the exclamation mark is used for emphasis and to signal an emotion – whether it be anger, joy, happiness or any of any other kind.

It is clear to him now how to use one in a letter, but in a document? He again goes over in his mind the tens of thousands of documents he has written that never had a single exclamation mark; he is certain he can't remember one.

The story lends itself very well to pointing out how a routine, factual existence is possible, with everything in the right place, well documented and well documentable, but devoid of any emotion such as anger, joy or jealousy. After this sleepless night the story's protagonist decides to go to his head of department and in the appointment diary where he has to express his wish to be seen, he writes his own name Yefim Perekladin and adds three exclamation marks. Chekhov concludes that as the clerk wrote the three marks, he was filled with delight, indignation, joy and rage. Pressing down hard on his pen, he exclaimed: "Take that, take that!" (Chekhov, 1999).

Post-Bion the very concept of reality has changed

Reality is that thing that needs to be dreamed in order for it to become thinkable and manageable. Here the analyst must go through a significant and painful mourning process. The analyst must set aside the reality quotient of the patient's communications – and only in this way can the analyst dream them and transform them into images and narratives.

A patient invents another personality that is "sold" to everyone as authentic: the patient is a member of the secret services, a Special Forces paratrooper, and is called upon to resolve international crises with a license to kill. "You are James Bond", I tell him at our first meeting. But what is the "fact" the patient did not know how to dream and transform? As the patient will come to say after a long analysis, it is the fact that the patient is a two-bit provincial lawyer, unattractive and alone. Lies have protected the patient from dreaming and alphabetizing a story that is too painful to accept.

As I said, the analyst is an enzyme capable of fostering the development of the tools for thinking, feeling and dreaming that we humans need to live.

Time to grow

Stefano is a child who was adopted when he was 3 and who at the age of 9 was brought in for consultation on account of his "violent and uncontainable behaviour".

His parents come to the first meeting on time; they are well dressed and speak with a posh accent. Their surname does not go unnoticed: "Mr and Mrs Canarini" (Canaries).

They immediately start talking about how Stefano is being "bullied" at school by older and more violent children, and they point out that he is constantly telling lies, committing petty theft and always hungry. Although they punish him severely, only slaps seem to be really effective, even if they later regret what they have done.

At this point, the analyst imagines that by some twist of fate a small hawk has arrived in the Canaries' nest that now subverts the whole system. The inevitable lie stems from the fact that Stefano is supposed to behave like a Canary when he is in fact an Eaglet. His rapacious hunger is part of the same theme.

Then immediately a second fantasy forms in the analyst's mind: some sheep have adopted a baby that turns out to be a wolf cub.

A steady stream of lies about identity, needs, instincts, rapacity, theft, hunger.

Not only that, but his "eagle-like" modalities have also been transmitted to the parents who, now "eagleized", beat him up.

These fantasies also accompany the analyst as he listens in subsequent meetings.

Even as early as their very first sessions, Stefano (incredibly enough) talks about *Dances with Wolves*, German shepherds, Dobermanns and Rottweilers.

The videogames he describes centre around bloody fights where throats are slashed and enemies killed. Then Fury appears, the horse from the television series. What is striking is also the absence of limits, which leads him to steal, to eat raw meat, to bite his companions. After one of his petty thefts, his mother gave him a slap, he kicked her, then . . . "I lost control. . . . It was anger, I don't know . . . I was afraid, then my dad beat me . . .".

Postscript

After re-reading this chapter several times I find myself back in possession of my two souls – the *continuist* and the *discontinuist*. Once again I have been prompted to think that the right measure of things lies in a constant oscillation between concepts, just like the back-and-forth between the different structures of the mind we call contiguous-autistic, paranoid-schizoid and depressive.

References

Bion, W.R. (1997). *Taming wild Thoughts*. London: Karnac.

Chekhov, A. (1999). The exclamation mark. In: *The Comic Stories* (pp. 131–135). Chicago: Ivan R. Dee.

Civitarese, G. (2014). *Truth and the Unconscious*. London: Routledge, 2016.

Ferro, A. (2009). Transformations in dreaming and characters in the psychoanalytic field. *The International Journal of Psychoanalysis*, 90:209–230.

Ferro, A. (2010). Navette per l'Inconscio: rêveries, trasformazioni in sogno, sogni. *Rivista di Psicoanalisi*, 56:615–634.

Grotstein, J.S. (2007). *A Beam of Intense Darkness*: *Wilfred Bion's Legacy to Psychoanalysis*. London: Karnac.

Chapter X

Ogden's parentheses, or the continuity between conscious and unconscious experience

The spontaneous reaction of many analysts, myself included, to the idea of pausing to reflect on the concept of the unconscious on the occasion of the SPI National Congress held in Taormina in 2010 was paradoxical, a mixture of irony and annoyance. It was as if we saw the topic as too vast or, on the other hand, as something that could be taken for granted and thus of little interest. At a second glance, however, none of this proved to be true. The concept of the unconscious, the cornerstone of psychoanalysis, lends itself very well to being marked off; also, it is not self-evident, since it can be described from very different theoretical perspectives; and lastly, if we manage to overcome our initial resistance, we realize that reflecting on our current way of conceiving the unconscious can become a profitable exercise because it entails clarifying the principles on which we all base our way of working with patients.

One of the most stimulating entry routes into this challenging theoretical terrain can be found in Thomas Ogden's (2009) recently published *Rediscovering Psychoanalysis. Thinking and Dreaming, Learning and Forgetting*. For some decades now, Ogden has been one of the most creative authors in psychoanalysis, and as such a member of a very select group. In order to approach this new work of his – precisely from the particular vantage point of the theory of the unconscious – I propose to start with a note on the author's writing style.

Parentheses

Each sentence Ogden writes is honed to achieve maximum possible clarity. Stripped clean of any jargon, his writing is both dense and evocative in the way only the words of poetry can be.

DOI: 10.4324/9781003279020-10

One characteristic feature of Ogden's style is his use of parentheses or brackets (a detail already noted by Akhtar, 1996). Parentheses have a reflexive (self-mirroring), supplementary (*nachträglich*) and non-essential or marginal character (like the waste products of the psyche). They could be removed without affecting the meaning of the rest of the sentence (and become indispensable only in stream-of-consciousness writing – for example as practiced by Faulkner). They are grammatically extraneous to the context into which they are inserted (and yet, by cutting into or leaving an imprint on the discourse, they complete its meaning).

Parentheses produce discontinuities, various layers of meaning and polyphonic effects (Mortara Garavelli, 2003). They are equivalent to those slight jolts that in Ogden's view help us apprehend the emergence of the unconscious as something that is not "below" or "behind" but rather inside the conscious, provided we know how to perceive them: ideas, memories, sudden and transitory bodily sensations, brooding worries, etc. They have the subtly intrusive quality of reverie and hint at its movement. They allude to the two (or more) conscious and unconscious voices that interlace to create a third that is more than their sum. They live in the moment of an almost imperceptible suspension of the trajectory of thought. They open up a space for a kind of reading (and listening) that takes a different orientation. They carve out new points of view. They also act as an implicit interpretation of what precedes them, and it is almost as if they assumed there was a dark (unconscious) core that needed to be illuminated with a further light effect. In short, the way Ogden uses parentheses – with great discretion and yet putting them in plain sight – is an embodiment in his writing of the very movement of thought and the continuity that exists between conscious and unconscious.

The relationship between conscious and unconscious experience

Rediscovering psychoanalysis then becomes a question of reconceiving the relationship between conscious and unconscious experience. This is the heading of the last section of the book which by its very position suggests that it contains the key to understanding the whole book. The chapter is dedicated to Searles, and here Ogden comments on the evident awareness of the continuity between conscious and unconscious experience to be found in that author's analytic work, going on to give a refined analysis of some clinical cases taken from some of his studies. These examples show how Searles manages with extraordinary sensitivity to "turn inside out" his awareness of his more refined emotional impulses in order to probe what is taking place on the invisible level of the transference-countertransference. Ogden attributes the paternity of this idea to Bion: "Bion recognized in his own work what Searles demonstrated in his clinical accounts, and used that recognition to revolutionize analytic theory by radically altering the topographic model" (Ogden, 2009, p. 152).

Ogden's remark interweaves several levels of discourse at the same time, because the principle of the permeability between conscious and unconscious experience is immediately put to use to shed light on the relationship that exists between these two authors and among psychoanalytic authors in general. Ogden sets up a dialogue between Searles and Bion, and then weighs in himself, joining in a conversation that has a dialectical thrust and that creates a third subject. This subject is no longer Bion, no longer Searles, but an entity that is made up of both the one and the other – and in which Ogden himself participates. The tone of the very next sentence renders the precise measure of this:

> Bion's alteration of the topographic model is nothing less than breathtaking in that it had been impossible, at least for me, to imagine psychoanalysis without the idea of an unconscious mind somehow separate from ('below') the conscious mind. The conscious and unconscious 'minds', for Bion, are not separate entities, but dimensions of a single consciousness.
>
> (*ibid.*)

It is not hard to imagine the sense of wonder and almost vertigo that Ogden must have felt at this moment. The personal comment contained in the word "breathtaking" points to a way of experiencing psychoanalysis that involves total intellectual and emotional investment; not reducing it to a set of algebraic theories, but constituting it as something personal and constantly rediscovered. Likewise, we can easily recognize elements of Ogden's personality that are already known to us from his other works: simplicity and complexity, respect for tradition and the courage to embrace new ideas that at first may even seem bizarre, balance, originality, delicacy, a profound sense of personal integrity, genuine and unaffected humility. Each one of Ogden's works is an impressive lesson in ethics, knowledge, technique, focus and style. Equally, however, his works also provide a lesson about the arrogance (which in one of his famous essays Bion links to the paranoid-schizoid position) that at times also characterizes controversies among analysts.

Bion's principles of mental functioning

In the light of the book's closing section, the centrality of this sixth chapter, dedicated to Bion's four principles of mental functioning, stands out even more. Here Ogden reveals to the reader the extent of Bion's influence on his own thinking. Likewise, he helps the reader gain a better grasp of the way in which he works his understanding of the Bionian revolution of the theory of the unconscious into the various spheres of the analyst's activity (clinical work, supervision, teaching, research).

In this superb section, Ogden explains how Bion's theory of thought is built on four pillars: the mind needs truth to grow ("Who am I? What is going on in my life?"); two minds[1] are required for someone to think their most disturbing thoughts; the capacity for thinking develops as a way of dealing with thoughts that have their origin in a person's most disturbing emotional experience; there is such a thing as the psychoanalytic function of the personality, and this function is carried out mainly through dreaming.

All four principles concern the individual's relationship to reality, a relationship Bion conceives of very differently from Freud (for whom the search for pleasure through the discharge of instinctual tension was at the centre of everything). Each of Bion's principles (which Ogden reformulates in his own language) begins "not with instinctual pressure but with lived emotional experience in the real world, and ends with thinking and feeling this experience" (*ibid.*, p. 91). For Freud, the unconscious has absolutely no interest in reality testing, while for Bion "without (unconscious) phantasies and without dreams you have not the means to think out your problems" (*ibid.*).

By need for truth, the prime and most fundamental principle of all, Bion means the subject's drive to attain a correct sense of reality, the feeling of being destined to think and learn from experience, the realization that having an adequate grasp of things is essential to psychological growth. The need to know the truth about one's existence constitutes the most fundamental stimulus for thought. In Bion's theory it is the only true motivational criterion the individual has and it plays the role that Freud on the other hand assigned to drives. The very essence of the developmental conflict lies in passing from magical thought (which is in fact never completely absent), the form of non-thought that eludes reality, to genuine thought that instead faces up to its radical otherness and tries to modify it. Mature thought differs from magical thought, from our most archaic fears; and its evolution depends on the capacity to put up with doubt and periods of waiting, as well as on the ability to keep up several vantage points on things. Having a single point of view, on the other hand, is tantamount to finding oneself potentially in a psychotic state.

For Bion, therefore, thought is a radically intersubjective experience, and the human unit is the couple (when things go well, the Oedipal function of the mind, that is, the paternal signifier, is also contained in the mother). Through projective identification, mother and child "think together"; the activity that we know as "thought", writes Bion, was originally projective identification. By engaging in this activity, the infant acquires an elementary and fragile sense of reality and develops its innate rudimentary ability to think (alpha function). On the intrapsychic level, the two minds become parts of the child's personality that converse with each other. Sometimes, however, this intrapsychic conversation is insufficient and the individual reaches the limit of his or her abilities. Then, in order to think about the most disturbing emotional experiences, the presence of a separate person becomes necessary (third principle). An individual may find himself in this condition as the result of trauma or because he has internalized not the alpha function but its reverse. This occurs when the negative emotions transmitted to the mother by means of projective identification bounce back without having been transformed, but rather with greater violence. The result is a form of thought in which there has been an erosion of the ability to make sense of experience by transforming sensoriality into pictograms (mostly, but not limited to, visual images) and by joining up the dream thoughts necessary to think and dream. Here we see why Bion's theory cannot be defined as relational.

The fourth principle postulates the existence of a psychoanalytic function of the personality (which Ogden sees as analogous to the inborn structure of natural language described by Chomsky). The main process for exercising this function is dreaming. Dreaming is thus equivalent to unconscious thinking or, one might rather say, it represents its main, albeit not exclusive, component. The adjective needs to be explained: "What makes this function of the personality 'psychoanalytic' is the fact that the psychological work is achieved to a large extent by means of viewing an emotional situation simultaneously from the perspective of the conscious and unconscious mind" (2009, p. 103). While for Freud it is a question of making the derivatives of the unconscious available to secondary conscious thought, for Bion, in order to grow the psychoanalytic function of the mind (essentially the ability to dream experience), that which was conscious must be made unconscious. As can be seen, this is a 180 degree change! The distinction between primary and secondary processes disappears. Dreaming does not spring from the difference between conscious and unconscious, but rather *creates* the difference itself. This is why Bion argues that the psychotic is unable to dream (to fall asleep or to wake up) and thus to differentiate between conscious and unconscious.

Thinking and dreaming

Let us now take a look at what Ogden creatively garners from Bion's influence on his thinking: in essence, he makes these principles his own, that is to say, he gives them a personal meaning. My impression is that, in "rediscovering" psychoanalysis, Ogden (and Bion before him) is pursuing the prime purpose of making us again (or more) sensitive to the potentially subversive discourse of the unconscious; causing us to be surprised by its productions, aside from the theoretical encrustations that have been added over time as a consequence of the inevitable tendency of institutions (including psychoanalytic ones) to close themselves off defensively; and forging tools that allow us to enter more closely into attunement with the truth of the unconscious. This is obviously an emotional truth; it is neither abstract nor absolute – a common misunderstanding – but rather synonymous with self-awareness, in other words, the ability to see oneself as one really is and to make use of emotional experience (Bion, 1962); and bearing in mind that in Bion's view it makes no sense to speak of emotion in isolation from a relationship.

So far we have been talking about the chapter in Ogden's book that deals with Bion's theory of thought. However, the book also includes an introduction and six other chapters, all of which (apart from two) had already been published in the *International Journal of Psychoanalysis*. Each in its own way seeks to address the consequences of a radical theoretical move, namely Bion's reconceptualization of the unconscious and, more specifically, his postulate of waking dream thought, arguably his most brilliant idea. This is a list of topics dealt with: the dream paradigm in sessions, supervision, teaching psychoanalysis, analytic style (above all, in Bion's clinical seminars), and re-readings of Loewald and Searles.

At the heart of Ogden's thought lies therefore the equation between thinking and dreaming, which he takes over from Bion but to which he gives even more prominence. His definition of it places the highest value on Freud's discovery of dream work (an important element of his continuity with Freud)[2] – which Lacan reformulates as a rhetoric of the unconscious – and at the same time capitalizes on Bion's amazing reversal of perspective: dreaming is

> the most free, most inclusive and most deeply penetrating form of psychological work of which human beings are capable . . . the principle medium through which we achieve human consciousness, psychological growth and the capacity to create personal, symbolic meaning from our lived experience.
>
> (Ogden, 2009, p. 104)

The patient's capacity to dream his or her experience, or rather to give it personal meaning, becomes the analytic pair's ability in the session to dream the emotional experience in progress, that is, to transform it into something new that the subject can assimilate. Dreaming a dream, at night or while awake, means being able to digest (symbolize) the emotional experience in progress. The product of this activity passes into memory and helps enhance a person's overall capacity to carry out the conscious, preconscious and unconscious psychological work that forms the basis of the ability to dream emotional experience. Just as the nutritional molecules absorbed during digestion serve the functioning of the digestive system itself and enable its development, so dreaming a dream and the potential capacity to perform unconscious psychological work are not the same thing, although the two processes are closely related. Unconscious thinking goes wider than dreaming the emotional experience of the moment; it includes it.

Reading the chapter on talking-as-dreaming is like taking in a breath of fresh air; one can feel the inexhaustible vitality and the still intact creative force of psychoanalysis. Dreaming is no longer seen as the process that leads from the unconscious to the conscious; on the contrary, dreaming serves to make "conscious lived experience available to the richer thought processes involved in unconscious psychological work" (*ibid.*). This is why the conversation that takes place in the session with the patient sometimes only has the taste of truth and reality when it is "talking-as-dreaming" – about films, books, sports and other subjects – something apparently superficial and non-analytic, to which is later added "talking about dreaming" – the moment of interactivity that follows after immersion in the virtual reality of the setting. Sometimes the analyst realizes what he or she is saying only after having said it. Only in retrospect does the analyst grasp the unconscious meaning of what has been said, only then can the analyst hear what a second, unexpected voice says (as in a parenthesis), which is added to the first, something the analyst did not yet know was within but for which he or she takes responsibility.

In "Talking-as-Dreaming", Ogden listens to the patient as if the patient were unconsciously commenting on what is happening moment by moment between himself or herself and the analyst. Making this evident to the patient would, however, mean interrupting the dream and obstructing the analytic pair's path towards emotional intimacy. When this situation occurs, the accord is not only symbolic but musical; it involves body and mind on a deep level and then translates into an experience of psychosomatic (re)integration. Emotional threads are woven together that expand the psychic container, which thus becomes capable of gradually encompassing ever more challenging contents. It is no longer so much a question of "making interventions" or "making interpretations". If the analyst communicates to the patient the understanding of the latter's words too soon, this potentially robs the patient of the opportunity of having one of the first experiences of dreaming in analysis and thus of approaching an emotional intensity and authenticity previously precluded to him – unless, that is, this understanding is part of a conversation that is fluid, genuine and presented with tact, respect and in conjectural form.

It is clear why, on the other hand, sticking only to facts, history, material reality, etc., can be a way of blinding oneself to the unconscious, confusing the emotional truth of the therapeutic relationship lived in the present time of the session with the presumed adherence of the historian to objective data (but then, suggests Bezoari [2010], one should use documents, other techniques, other tools, etc.). Instead, as Benjamin writes, the now is "the most intimate image of the past" (1966, p. 144). With Bion (Ogden) we pass from reservoir memory to dream memory, "the stuff of analysis"

(Bion, 1970, pp. 70). The most valuable factor in illuminating history too is the emotional truth of the moment. As Ogden comments, the patient not only says what has happened but shows it. However, while the first element (the emotional truth of the encounter, emotional unison, ultimately the primordial form of consensuality and original symbolization or *Bejahung*) is essential for therapy, strictly speaking the second (biographical reconstruction) is ancillary. Meltzer (1984) shares this view, referring to it as a secondary effect of analysis. It is obvious that the greater the integration of the subject, the more the patient will also be able to fill in the gaps in her life story, the more solid will be her feeling of herself and the experience of the continuity of her existence.

It would be incorrect to say that Ogden idealizes talking-as-dreaming. He is well aware, in fact, that these moments that are perceived as happier are often the result of much work and that therefore they stand in a dialectical relationship with less inspired and more ordinary modes of interaction. Equally, he never loses sight of the importance of respecting the setting ("[m]ore, not less, attention to the analytic frame is required", Ogden, 2009, p. 30) and the basic asymmetry of the analytic relationship ("Otherwise, the patient is deprived of an analyst and of the analytic relationship that he needs"). The asymmetry stems from the very nature of the treatment device (which, as a "device", implies a process of subjectivation, Agamben, 2006, p. 19) and presupposes, in Loewald's words, the differential of professional experience and emotional maturity between analyst and patient.

Psychoanalytic supervision

The third chapter focuses on psychoanalytic supervision. The opening salvo, as is so often the case with Ogden, is memorable.[3]

As if it were the most obvious thing in the world, we read that the supervisory relationship is one of two forms of human relatedness invented by Freud that had not previously existed. In this way Ogden attributes to it a value in itself as a human achievement and an experiential depth that perhaps we would not have realized before hearing his authoritative and persuasive voice on the subject. Not to the same extent. Here too, central to Ogden's conception of interaction in the supervisory relationship, as well as to analysis itself, is the awareness of its unconscious dimension and its permeability vis-à-vis conscious experience. The difficulties experienced by the supervisee reappear in the narration the supervisee creates out of the interaction with the patient; they are not only communicated consciously, but also relived in the supervisory relationship.

Teaching

The fourth chapter looks at the topic of teaching, which Ogden interprets in a comment on important articles by some classical analytic authors. In the seminars he conducts with his students, and which he sees as collective dream experiences, he asks them to read the text aloud so as to appreciate the effect of the sound of the words and the rhythm of each sentence as something that inevitably contributes to organizing their meaning. In this way he tries to tune in to the "unconscious" of the text, with its performative and musical quality. Attention is paid to the experience of reading aloud just as in the session it is directed at the experience taking place between patient and analyst. In Ogden's view, re-reading an author's work is never an academic exercise. It can never be reduced to the extraction of arid and lifeless meanings, to a set of rules and precepts; rather, properly speaking it is an act of "re-dreaming". Eschewing other forms of mediation, once again Ogden makes the reader engage directly with the experience he is talking about, and thus communicates the essence of what it means to get in touch with the unconscious dimension of the mind.

Rediscovering an author implies, so to speak, creating a new one. Reading (writing) is a creative act; it is also about composing, transforming the discovery made by another into one's own discovery. This does not mean betraying an author's ideas, because showing creative infidelity is the truest, most intimate and profound form of understanding. It is easy to say what infidelity entails: each time something is created that belongs both to the reader and the chosen author. What Ogden says about Searles and Bion also applies to Ogden himself. One need only look at the book's closing words:

> It is impossible to say to what extent Bion was influenced by Searles or Searles by Bion. . . . Nonetheless, what I hope to have demonstrated is that Searles's work is enriched conceptually by a knowledge of Bion's work and Bion's work is brought more fully to life experientially by a familiarity with that of Searles.
>
> (Ogden, 2009, p. 153)

It is clear that this implies – as Ogden attributed to Searles with regard to the interaction between supervisor and supervisee – "a form of bringing the entirety of oneself, the full depth and breadth of emotional responsiveness to bear not only on an analytic relationship" (*ibid.*, pp. 44), but this is also true in other areas where the analyst operates.

Significantly, then, the authors that Ogden studies and teaches (those he converses with) are all chosen from among those who have felt more than others the tension between tradition and revolution, between influence and the urge to leave behind the "conventional psychoanalytic knowledge" (*ibid.*, p. 53) of their time: Loewald, Winnicott, Bion, Searles (with the recent addition of Fairbairn). In this sense, it is emblematic that he devotes a chapter to Loewald's original conception of the Oedipus complex as a drive for emancipation from parents. The choice is insightful and come across as a warning issued to anyone who is interested in picking up Freud's legacy not so as to lock it away in a museum, but rather to bring it to life.

Notes

1 The second principle could also be expressed in the words of Kojève (1947, p. 43), the philosopher through whom Ogden absorbed Hegel's lesson about the intersubjective matrix of identity: "If they are to be *human*, they must be at least *two* in number".
2 Even though, strictly speaking, the two bear different signs: for Freud the dream disguises latent thoughts, for Bion it creates meaning.
3 One might look again, for example, at the beginning of *Subjects of Analysis* (1994, p. 1):

> It is too late to turn back. Having read the opening words of this book, you have already begun to enter into the unsettling experience of finding yourself becoming a subject whom you have not yet met, but nonetheless recognize.

References

Agamben, G. (2006). *Che cos'è un dispositivo?* Roma: Nottetempo.
Akhtar, S. (1996). *Subjects of Analysis* (T. Ogden, Ed.) (p. 230). Northvale, NJ: Jason Aronson, 1994. *International Journal of Psychoanalysis*, 77:625–628.
Benjamin, W. (1966). *Sul concetto di storia.* Turin: Einaudi, 1997.
Bezoari, M. (2010). "Dream-like memory". https://www.spiweb.it/wp-content/uploads/2018/03/2ok-6-2-6.dibattito-sulla-ricostruzione-a-cura-di-f.-carnaroli.pdf (accessed: 23/06/2019).

Bion, W.R. (1962). *Learning from Experience*. London: Tavistock.

Bion, W.R. (1970). *Attention and Interpretation: A Scientific Approach to Insight in Psycho-Analysis and Groups*. London: Tavistock.

Kojève, A. (1947). *Introduction to the Reading of Hegel: Lectures on the Phenomenology of Spirit*. Ithaca, NY: Cornell University Press, 1980.

Meltzer, D. (1984). *Dream-Life: A Re-Examination of the Psycho-Analytical Theory and Technique*. Strathtay, Scotland: Clunie Press.

Mortara Garavelli, B. (2003). *Prontuario di punteggiatura*. Bari: Laterza.

Ogden, T.H. (2009). *Rediscovering Psychoanalysis: Thinking and Dreaming, Learning and Forgetting*. London: Routledge.

Chapter XI

Reality and fictions

People (story), internal objects (unconscious fantasies), characters (casting)

I believe that the specific nature of the psychic dimension consists in the act of relinquishing external reality, facts, people and history, and turning rather to a *transformative fiction* that grants access to emotions, narratives and characters.

The "analyst at work" (and henceforth when I say analyst and/or patient I will always mean "analyst and patient at work in an appropriate setting") must forgo external reality or rather must accept the loss of external reality in order to enter the de-concretized, de-constructed and then if possible *re-dreamed* world, as Thomas Ogden (2009) suggests when he states that the purpose of analysis is to help the patient have the dreams that the patient has not been able to have by alone and which have become symptoms that can only be dispelled if they are "dreamed".

James Grotstein (2007) expresses an identical concept, albeit formulated differently, when he says that the human mind is at one and the same time something that continually works through stimuli and defences against "O" (truth, ultimate reality, facts, beta elements), and that all we can do is *transform into fiction – mythologize –* our perception, our experience of truth ("O"). This is made possible by the transit of O through column 2 of the Grid, the column of lies but also of dreams, which are also lies about "O".

There is a beautiful poem by Wisława Szymborska titled "Conversation with a Stone". The speaker asks a stone for permission to enter inside it but the stone refuses; he will never be able to enter. It would not help even if his sight were heightened to the point of becoming all-seeing (omniscience), because he lacks the notion of taking part. The "fact", the "event", the "real datum", the "stone" of symptoms or reality must, at the entrance to column 2, encounter the analyst's ability to take part, which I would define as the ability to share the patient's manifest story or "thing".

DOI: 10.4324/9781003279020-11

This will allow access into row 2, where the lithotripter will be found that consists of the analyst's de-constructive, de-concretizing and re-dreaming capacity. (For simplicity's sake, I will often speak of analyst and patient while implicitly what I am referring to will always be the "analytic field" as something new and different from the sum of its constituent parts; essentially what happens in row 2 happens at some place in the field.)

Following "taking part" (unison), what come into play are the *active tools* of mythopoesis, in other words, the alpha function, the capacity for reverie (basic reverie, flash reverie, construction reverie, transformation into dream, transformation into play, the dream, Ogden's talking-as-dreaming; Ferro, 2008, 2009; Bolognini, 2010).

Alongside these active tools we also have what I would term the *basic atmospheres* necessary for transformations to take place. These basic atmospheres are produced by the oscillation between negative capability and selected fact (CN ↔ FS), between the contiguous-autistic, paranoid-schizoid and depressive positions (PCA ↔ PS ↔ D), and between container and contained (♀↔♂).

The purpose of analysis (beyond what we already know about removing the veil of repression, working on integrating split-off parts, insight, having the ego take the place of the id, etc.) consists above all in the development of these active tools and the development of atmospheres conducive to transformation. One point of entry into this description is, for example, to look at how the continual "casting" of characters (Ferro, 2009) turns a "person" in row 2 into a "character" in the analysis, or rather an affective hologram that is born out of what the field needs to express at any given moment.

There is one particular point regarding which there is a certain difference between me and the authors I see as being closest to me – that is, Ogden, Grotstein and Green – and that concerns the strong presence of the concept of field as developed by the Barangers (1961–1962) and a number of South American psychoanalysts, and then made even more complex by fertile coupling with Bion's thinking (1962, 1963, 1965). According to this concept, the internal groups within analyst and patient produce in the consulting room a cast of characters, who I have termed "affective holograms", and these are the result of the *transformation into dream* of what is said, acted out and experienced by the analyst's and the patient's mind. This latter is to be conceived of as a kind of group mind that de-concretizes or de-realizes communications by transforming them into dream scenes that "live inside the consulting room" and bring about the development of tools for thinking.

It is as if Ogden's (1994) "analytic third" were somehow diluted into a dream narrative of the functioning of the two minds. These progressively cast the characters they need in order to activate the dream that must be cared for and that must also be the first thing to bring to life.

On the question of Botella's (2002) cardinal concept of "figurability", I would say that it still alludes in some way to shreds of history (possibly mental history), where the concept of reverie refers to something that, for the most part at least, relates to the current functioning of the minds involved.

The central point to underline is that what happens in the analytic dialogue is a process of making "psychological" what had hitherto been chaotic and meaningless content.

As I was saying earlier, Grotstein (2007) maintains that our task should be to transform our perception, our experience of truth ("O"), into fiction. This leads me to reflect both on Bion's (1965) *Transformations* and on the chapter titled "Transformations" in Grotstein's book (2007), as well as on the journey that each "fact" must undertake in column 2 of the Grid in order to become alphabetized.

The continual re-dreaming process carried out by the field or by the patient and which signals that the analysis might "go off course" or be approaching submerged rocks, recalls Joseph Conrad's story "The Secret Sharer". The young captain of a sailing vessel helps a man come on board his ship and hides him in his cabin. At a certain point during the voyage, the ship is in danger of running aground on some rocks, but the stowaway saves the ship from disaster by throwing his hat into the water, thus helping the captain understand the swirl of the currents and save the ship.

The dream-making process is even more complex and less circumscribed, and it concerns the whole session and the dream-like journey through it: the session becomes a dream produced by the two minds that is continually being adjusted to allow for narratives and transformations to take the place of what is "not yet thinkable".

Thinking thoughts, living emotions, living the terror we at times feel, taking upon ourselves the suffering of others, getting into contact with our own inner creativity and that inside our patients and letting it emerge are perhaps good enough reasons for living, albeit in the full awareness of the insignificance of human existence.

I would also add that if we could accept Lucretius's contention that human beings are a freak of nature, and if we were aware of the terror that this generates in us (which is all the greater the more we deny it), then perhaps we could do – as Bion reminds us – what British and German troops at the front did on Christmas Day: play football in no man's land (Grotstein, 2007).

If we could play with the non-sense of life, perhaps to the horror of all the high-ranking fundamentalists, we might be able to open windows of awareness and peace.

If a female patient were to talk about abuses or mistreatment she had suffered, our way of listening could take the direction of de-concretizing, de-constructing and, as soon as possible, re-dreaming so as to reconstruct a narrative that is different from (and more tolerable than) the facts of the case: for example, we might try to reflect on the (perhaps uncontainable) emotions the patient feels abused by, or on what kind of a relationship with the analyst or with other potential identities of the field might have led to this.

Diluting facts into narrative sequences makes it possible to metabolize "facts" that were initially undigested and indigestible.

It may be worth recalling that there are two modes of creativity that take us towards narration: firstly, the way in which sensoriality is "picto-graphed" by forming mind-specific pictograms, and secondly, the way in which these are narrated in different narrative sequences.

There is a clear difference between, on the one hand, unconscious, shared fantasies – which I would say are common to the species as a whole (primal fantasies) – and, on the other, the sequences of pictograms (which go to form waking dream thought) that are specific to each mind or ana-lytic couple at work or to each analytic field that comes to life.

Any possible narrativistic slide can be avoided by paying attention to the indications the field continually provides directly through the patient's mouth and through the mouth of other characters, and sometimes also through the analyst's reverie and countertransference dreams. Typically, these occur when the Maginot line that marks the confines of the field gets buried under emotional turbulence.

What I envisage is a kind of psychoanalysis that looks to the develop-ment of functions for thinking, dreaming and feeling, and does not simply tackle repressed representations and split-off aspects of the personality; its focus will no longer be on the discovery or rediscovery of something buried or avoided, but rather on future meanings opened up by the field, even including the paradoxical transformational potential of "memories" of events that never happened and are in fact the precipitate of current experiences lived in the session and then backdated.

I would emphasize that beta elements, sensoriality, the facts the patient has not been able to dream despite the analyst's best efforts to modulate the field, burst onto the field and take no prisoners. The field is a hyper-receptive absorber of emotional turbulence that has not yet been alphabet-ized. What complicates things is that the analyst's subjectivity, turbulence (and defences against it) also go to constitute the field, which will there-fore always be specific to that pair.

Characters will enter the field that do not come from narratives based on external reality but by means of the "casting" process the field requires for it to express certain emotions: they are characters who are thus "abducted" from other realities so as to make it possible to experience and articulate the reality of the field, albeit in a fictional manner.

In my view, while we are in analysis and if an analysis is to make sense, there is nothing that cannot be said to have a rightful place in the consult-ing room and in the dream field co-produced by patient and analyst when the setting is in working order.

Understood in this way, the field looks more towards meanings to be generated and a future that starts from the here and now, as well as towards possible evolutions, including the rewriting of a different story.

Casting the characters

Or to put it another way: finding and bringing into the field the characters that are necessary to continue the dream or narration.

A monster daughter

Eleonora begins the Monday session by talking about the hatred she feels for her husband and how she wishes him dead because he is "lazy, arro-gant, disagreeable". *She then recounts a dream in which she dreamt of beating him to death.* The analyst, seeing the patient's tears, hands her a tissue.

She goes on to speak about her daughter Daria, who "now that she has put on so many pounds is a monster, really overweight, covered in pimples . . . .".

Who are the main characters and how should we think of them? How does the "casting" take place?

One character is "hate", something extremely violent and uncontainable that is activated inside her. Another character is "the husband", who we could think of as the alias of the female therapist and who is hated in part because she is lazy (she did not work last weekend). Then we have "the tears" and finally "the handkerchief" (this character also stands for the ability to receive and "dry" the patient's suffering).

After this cleansing operation (wiping away tears and hatred), Daria appears, or rather the way in which the patient sees herself as monstrous and very fat because she is "swollen with hatred" and pain.

"All" the characters who have been cast in their roles without there being any correspondence with external or historical reality should be understood as functions of the field. Each character is like some kind of goods wagon, an excipient that serves as the vehicle for the "active principle" the field needs to express at that moment. In short, the characters become expressive modes of functioning present in the field.

Thus, each patient strives to find a character that corresponds to what he/she or the field urgently needs to express.

But another character is also "the dream", and through the dream not only does the patient indicate content (anger and desire for revenge) but also that there is a field capable of mentalizing, of course in the sense of the word as used by Grotstein (2009), Ogden (2009) and myself (2009): the long transformative journey through column 2 and row 3 of Bion's Grid.

Characters in search of an author and authors in search of characters

The eastern European prostitute

Filippo experiences his wife Luciana's sexual rejection of him as extremely problematic. After she had turned him away for the umpteenth time, he went to an eastern European prostitute, with whom he had also chatted. The wife explains that she doesn't want to have sex because she is afraid the children in the room next door might hear the noise they are making.

Filippo has a dream in which he is in possession of a platinum – high-value – credit card. He comments on this dream by saying that what he needs to do to avoid falling into the depression he finds himself in is to regain the feeling that he is of "value", as opposed to taking "cannabis" (an extramarital affair and some exciting work situations).

Let's now try to depict this in diagram form, first adding however that Filippo experienced a new moment of despair when his wife turned him down again (saying "Why don't you go to a prostitute? For me the important thing is that you don't have an emotional relationship with another woman").

DIAGRAM OF CHARACTERS

Depression	Cannabis	Prostitute
Children	Platinum card	Extra-marital relationship
Filippo	Wife	?
?	?	?

The lower part of the diagram, with the question marks, is open to developments and the casting of possible new characters.

The box I would like to deal with is the one labelled "Wife", who can be viewed from many different points of view:

• The wife is a person who has her own psychology and problems that could be investigated, and Filippo must be enabled to enter into dialogue with them;
• The wife is an internal object, a residue, for example, of a cold and rejecting mother ("I can never believe that a beautiful woman I like would want to have a relationship with me", Filippo says in one session);
• The wife could be Filippo's way of casting a character who has a phobia of sex that relates to infantile aspects that must be protected, or a phobia of any intimacy that goes beyond the level of simple affection. This would also, or above all, be a problem that Filippo himself is unaware of having.

The story could be rewritten by changing some of the ephemeral data, the plot, and leaving the *fabula* unaltered.

Another way of further developing the "wife" box would be to see it as the casting of an autistic-Aspergerian – or perhaps rather "a-relational" – aspect inside Filippo of which is not aware.

Wife
Autistic a-relational aspect

Viewed under an even stronger magnifying glass, the "wife" could stand for another mode of functioning of Filippo's, unknown to him (except tangentially, when he says "when I make a move on a woman who interests me, I always expect to be rejected"), that is, a part of him that forestalls rejection by being the person who rejects, a sort of pre-emptive anaesthesia of possible pain.

> An aspect that prevents rejection by exposing itself to being rejected
>> Corresponds to one mind's experiences of the other with more $\male$
> than $\female$

If the degree of magnification is turned up even further (this remains as an unanalyzed or unanalyzable part), this might correspond to the sense of

> Finiteness and loneliness of greater intensity than the feelings
>> that dwell in every person's mind

The task to be faced during the next stage of work will be to see whether what we have in the "Wife" box can be deconstructed by casting new characters that will come to occupy the other potential boxes further down the diagram.

Similar work to that done relative to the "wife" box can be carried out for every other box.

But to make transformation possible, everything must enter the field; the "wife" must become an emotional hologram. The extent to which this is possible will depend on Fillipo and the qualities of the analyst's mind. To what extent will the latter be occluded or available? To what extent can the problem of rejection/relationship/intimacy live as a problem of the field? How can it be de-concretized and dreamed?

Is one possible dream that of a Yeti being rejected by an explorer it has fallen in love with? Might some kind of negative Tarzan/Jane pair-function or – (T/J) appear? At this point, how might this constellation – (T/J) be transformed into +(T/J), where emotional "coupling" would be tolerated and even desired?

Thus far I have omitted to emphasize that column 2 at some point intersects with row C of Bion's Grid (the sequence of alpha elements, dreams, myths) and that this intersection box (C2) is very special because this is where the maximum number of transformations occur.

Casting/reverie/transformations

If a very inhibited (self-hibernating) patient talks about a catafalque, what spontaneously catches my attention is the "falque/falcon" element – something that is extremely vital but is locked up or asleep inside a *claustrum*. I don't need to tell the patient this, but from that moment on I will look for a way to tune *into* the "falcon" and *with* the "falcon".

Similarly, I am very much drawn to what I have called "semantic nests", in other words, sites in the discourse that contain high communicative potential.

If at a certain point a hypothesis of abuse were to develop, the vertex I would take is to ask myself in what way I might have been an abuser or in what respect "the falcon" can be (have been?) abusive.

After all, what belongs to a reality external to analysis, either historical or current, can be transformed only to the extent that it comes to inhabit the analytic field.

If at some point in the analysis a "classmate" the patient had felt bullied by were to enter the session, for me and for as long as the analysis makes sense or as long as the stability of the setting makes sense, it could only be considered a function adopted somewhere in the field and acted out by the patient (as a disturbing potential identity) or by myself (as a disturbing presence for the patient).

If an experienced female analyst finds herself cutting short a session with a male patient who suffers from a certain mutism, I would necessarily think of silent abuse that the analyst is suffering that makes her try to remove the abused "container" (herself) from the abusive "contained".

Lava crown

I remember a drawing by a little girl that depicted the trunk and crown of a tree and which immediately put me in mind of an erupting volcano gushing lava. After a further two years of therapy, she came up with another drawing of a landscape as seen from an open window that contained numerous small trees with "lava crowns". The proto-emotional volcano had been broken down into lots of containable small volcanoes, as if a "destorming" of the storm of beta elements had been made possible which transformed them into discrete and therefore thinkable emotional clusters.

In conclusion, I would like to reiterate that the "psychic dimension" and the "group mind of the field" imply a relinquishing of reality and a coming to terms with its loss *during the session* to the benefit of a *newborn fictional reality*. The capacity to achieve unison, the constituent parts of the atmosphere conducive to transformation, the active tools that enable it are what make it possible to play out the very serious "game of psychoanalysis", which is at times painful, but at other times also pleasurable. The path from O to K – as with the path from knowledge to experience or from learning to growth – is in some ways a path "paved with lies". But often it is the only one we can afford, apart perhaps from some rare moments of insight or catastrophic transformation into O.

So reality must be dreamed for it to be narrated. It was Bion who said that the "facts" must be dreamed to find the way to thought. It is true that sometimes reality wins out over dreams, but in these cases the analysis is suspended, against the day when the conditions that will allow play to restart are re-established.

The cube

At the end of the session, Carla, a young patient who comes to four sessions a week, tells me about a dream her boyfriend had one night he slept at her house (irrespective of who had the dream, I regard it as relevant to our analytic space): *she forced him to go on a trip to Paris but then sent him out on a dangerous and very difficult path overlooking the sea. Later he found himself in a cube that was travelling along an already laid-out road that would occasionally widen, come to an end and then start up again in the direction of a new stopping-place, and so on: it was a journey that had to be undertaken but afforded absolutely no pleasure.*

The patient herself commented: "But why does my boyfriend think that our life together will be precarious, dangerous and above all a nightmare (the Italian word for which is "incubo"; see earlier), passing through stages that had already been laid out and offering nothing in the way of beauty?". In this way she gave voice to her doubts about the various stages of life (living together, getting married, having children) that she did not yet feel ready for because she had not enjoyed any of the spaces of freedom that were still closed off to her and struck fear into her. Yet giving this up clearly caused her a degree of depression. Here too the patient presented a discrepancy between the real time of her actual age and the time of her age as she experienced it.

Time stands still

At her first consultation, a woman aged about 40 tells me that she is tormented by the idea that her children might fall ill. She then says that she has been living inside this terror for nine years; or rather, it would be better to say that she *hasn't* been living for nine years. When her second child was born, things got worse. She waits anxiously for any sign of a cold that might be the harbinger of a fever – and then who knows what might happen.

I tell her that she seems to see her children as shackles on her feet. Surely, I say, there must be times when she feels the desire to free herself from them or to escape. "Of course I do! And I can easily understand those mothers who kill their own children. Cinemas, theatres and admirers have all disappeared from my life since my children were born".

"You must feel like a doctor on call in an intensive care unit", I say.

She goes on to acknowledge that time stopped nine years ago: she is 45, but she feels no older than 22 or 23.

I tell her that it is understandable she should think that the death of her children (whom she loves) would enable her to leave her maximum security prison and help her find a way to liberate the part of herself that longs for "a reckless life, a life where the night is always young" (this is a line from a very famous song by the Italian singer-songwriter Vasco Rossi).

She immediately responds to this theme and starts talking about all the things she desires and which she thinks she must now give up forever! Time stopped when she was 23 and hasn't moved on; at 23 (mentally) she finds herself shouldering the weight and responsibility of a family that only a woman in the prime of her adulthood could handle.

There follows the long story of her mother's illness, which had, as it were, frozen time. She then talks about a trip to New York that she had planned in the past and would still be keen to go on. I tell her that all she needs to do is go along to a travel agent's to get a ticket/analysis that will allow her to fix her personal time zones and make up for lost time.

This applies even more when a patient presents with "zero characters", in which case the characters will have to start germinating in a kind of desert.

How can boredom, silence, repetitiveness or extreme stupidity turn into *La Strada, Crime and Punishment, The Silence of the Lambs* or *Anna*

Karenina? Some examples can be found in clinical cases I have described at greater length elsewhere (Ferro, 2002, 2003).

There are analyses in which we start with characters we imagine as leading players and who then either confirm themselves as such or leave the scene completely; alternatively, other unexpected and unpredictable characters may make an appearance.

With other analyses, where trust is needed, it is like being in a western where the difficulty lies in herding together cattle that are scattering in all directions, steering them to the river, and getting them to cross over to thinkability – and later to make steaks, hamburgers and fillets out of them.

The unthinkable world

What is Anna's unthinkable world? One "adequate" session follows another. Anna is the brilliant patient every analyst wishes for.

But who is Anna? What are Anna's other possible worlds? For the moment she is an accomplished actress ready and able to play the part for which she trained in the Actor's Studio: "the excellent patient".

What untapped potential might eventually express itself? It might include the equally valid possibility – like the lesson Poe teaches us in "The Purloined Letter" – that Anna is only fully Anna and nothing else!

I am reminded of the *Star Trek* series that at a certain point came to be populated with physically weird inhabitants from other worlds: we must become inured to these "monsters" if and when they exist, as Bion does in *A Memory of the Future*.

So, I would suggest we lend an ear to what the patient says, does or feels, but keep the other ear (or eye) always open to the Nativity Scene of something previously unthinkable or unimagined. Not all patients will ask this of us, but if they so wish, they have that right. Perhaps this is the difference between analysis and psychotherapy.

Analysis is a voyage of adventure, like going in search of the source of the Nile, or following in the footsteps of Indiana Jones. Those who undertake it must have a taste for travel and discovery. Psychotherapy is like saying: I'm sick and I want to get better but let's keep the workload down to a minimum.

There is nothing stopping us from "switching" from one track to another at any time.

The self is made up of "many selves", and normally some dominate over others; I would add, however, "for now". Other potentials might come to life – as in *I Am Legend* – at night, in the dark, and try to devour the dominant identities.

The sun at your back

A patient describes *dreaming of the man on reception at the residential hotel where she spends her summer holidays: he wears his sunglasses the wrong way round, that is to say, at the back of his head*. I immediately think that the sun is behind him. But what does that mean? Does he feel the imminent approach of sunset or does he at times feel blinded by my interventions that are too bright/blinding for the back of his head?

I have no way of knowing this right away; we'll have to see which itinerary wins out.

Meanwhile, we can see one of the functions of dreams: they are *ghost-busters* or rather a tool to help us cast characters that would otherwise be beyond reach. The dream introduced the character "man with sunglasses at the back of his head"; our dream of the session will help us to situate and connect with this character, and to splice together the film co-directed with the patient.

If then, following a story about a mix-up between real and plastic coins (tokens) in a supermarket, the analyst told a joke that brought in the character of a "con artist", this might set in motion a sequence in which someone wants to stop his nape from being exposed to painful sights (or "con it out of" this sight). But this is only one of many possible hypothetical developments. If the patient then said "today my father took me out to lunch, then the sun came out", this might confirm the hypothesized plot (someone has transformed sensoriality into food) and the meteorological conditions of the session would promise fine weather.

Thus, by trial and error, by the constant adjustment and re-adjustment carried out by different edits, the dream of the session comes to life with a character that might be cast by the patient's dream, or have its origin in a reverie, or be directly introduced by the patient. In other words, first you have to do the shopping (the casting) and then the cooking – and *this* is the dream of the session.

Before the Christmas break, a patient says she has "sprained her foot" and is in a lot of pain – thus pain enters the session. She then adds that she "twisted" her ankle or rather she says that unknowingly "she was" twisted by the separations that cause her so much pain. Of course, all this will have to find a way to be embodied in a story that will go from a zero level of transformation ("You are telling me you are angry and in pain"), to Tn transformative levels depending on the extent to which the director or editor function has been activated. Above all, the important thing is whether it will be able to develop the micro/macro mythopoetic capacity of the field beyond the content itself. Sometimes it is also possible to simply decipher or fit together the pieces of a puzzle, but in these cases a lot of work has already been done and the characters are just waiting to be inserted into a narrative plot.

In intensive care

Laura begins the session by talking about her well-being, the fact that she feels good. She then mentions two consultations she has given in an intensive care unit, one to a boy waiting for a heart transplant and the other to a girl waiting for a lung transplant.

In these cases, I believed that I had enough information (the patient had already provided some "dream sequences") and so I felt I could say that on the one hand I was reminded of a cheerful advertisement for a healthy snack for children, on the other I deduce that she was having problems of the heart and that she felt suffocated by something, that something was preventing her from taking deep breaths. At this point it is the patient herself who goes on to develop these two themes that seemed to be waiting only for a way to become available that would enable her to break down and express her dissatisfaction and concerns about her choices in matters of the heart and also her needs for freedom and autonomy.

References

Bion, W.R. (1962). *Learning from Experience*. London: Tavistock.

Bion, W.R. (1963). *Elements of Psycho-Analysis*. London: Heinemann.

Bion, W.R. (1965). *Transformations: Change from Learning to Growth*. London: Heinemann.

Bolognini, S. (2010). Secret passages towards the unconscious. *The Italian Psychoanalytic Annual*, 5:75–87, 2011.

Botella, C., & Botella, S. (2002). *The Work of Psychic Figurability: Mental States Without Representation*. London: Routledge, 2005.

Ferro, A. (2002). *Seeds of Illness, Seeds of Recovery: The Genesis of Suffering and the Role of Psychoanalysis*. London: Routledge, 2004.

Ferro, A. (2003). Marcella from explosive sensoriality to the ability to think. *Psychoanalytic Quarterly*, LXXII:183–200.

Ferro, A. (2008). The patient as the analyst's best colleague: Transformation into dream a and narrative transformation. *The Italian Psychoanalytical Annual of Rivista di Psicoanalisi*:199–205.

Ferro, A. (2009). Transformations in dreaming and characters in the psychoanalytic field. *The International Journal of Psychoanalysis*, 90:209–230.

Grotstein, J.S. (2007). *A Beam of Intense Darkness: Wilfred Bion's Legacy to Psychoanalysis*. London: Karnac.

Grotstein, J.S. (2009). Dreaming as a 'curtain of illusion': Revisiting the 'royal road' with Bion as our guide. *International Journal of Psychoanalysis*, 90:733–752.

Ogden, T.H. (1994). The analytic third: Working with intersubjective clinical facts. *International Journal of Psychoanalysis*, 75:3–19.

Ogden, T.H. (2009). *Rediscovering Psychoanalysis: Thinking and Dreaming, Learning and Forgetting*. London: Routledge.

Chapter XII

Internet and simultaneous life

Pathologies caused by the Internet?

I cannot recall any of my patients ever having suffered from problems caused by the Internet. Quite the opposite: I have had patients who have the Internet to thank for successfully overcoming inhibitions and establishing new emotional bonds by making intelligent use of chatlines, dating sites and Facebook. It would be easy to list all the exciting novelties that the Internet has brought with it and to rebut the criticisms levelled at it one by one. Contrary to McLuhan's view of television, it could be said that the medium is not the message; if that were true then it would also apply to the car, the telephone, the telegraph. What makes the difference is the way the medium is used. Therefore, it is difficult or perhaps premature to judge whether the Internet in itself promotes new forms of pathology or whether all it does is to give a further opportunity to those that already existed to manifest in a different form. My aim here, however, is to attempt to describe a specific aspect of this technology that I think can best be linked to the addictive diseases that have been reported in the literature, namely, the experience of temporality on the Internet which I would sum up in the concept of "simultaneity".

As we know, we use the word "simultaneous" to talk about an event that is synchronous or contemporary or that happens at the same time as another. Simultaneity on the Internet means that the instant I have a desire I can satisfy it. We now have the impression that everything happens in real time. I want a book and I order it on Amazon. It is true that then the book actually arrives and that the action is not illusory; nonetheless the sending of the order ("order"!) has something "hallucinatory" about it. With the one-click function, I don't even have to enter my password or any other data normally required.

DOI: 10.4324/9781003279020-12

The journals I subscribe to are still delivered to my home in the traditional printed format, but by then I will have already read the interesting articles – and even then, not in the digital edition but in the early view format.

I want to see a film and now I can stream it online. More often than not, I download it from the net using peer-to-peer programs or illegal servers located in countries beyond the reach of our laws. The net thus transforms me into a virtual pirate and highlights the violent nature of this act of appropriation, the defiance of any law, third party or father. I think of a place I'd like to visit and I no longer need to go there in person because Google Maps provides me with Street View and I can browse through images of it on my computer monitor (Baudrillard's vision of the world reduced to a simulacrum has never been so true).

Video games are now interactive and involve multiple players in real time. Playing together doesn't imply knowing each other first or being friends (although that's not always the case). The only thing that unites users is that they are surfing the Internet at the same time, like so many dots on the web. Not to mention chat rooms, virtual sex, online dating sites, etc.

Memory takes up residence in electronic clouds, at least the memory that is fixed on paper or is physically present on hard disks.

Photographs disappear precisely when in digital format they become infinite due to the almost zero cost and because the photographic eyes from which we never detach ourselves have multiplied (it's no coincidence that the brand name for Apple's state-of-the-art display is Retina). But we no longer print them and we no longer contemplate them as we used to do with those yellowed pieces of card that magically helped us retrieve things from our past. We accumulate images that are bereft of the poetic patina wrought by time, and which no longer nurture us.

We hand over our identity and privacy to the various social networks – Twitter, Facebook, LinkedIn – and these masters of the net sometimes use our data for commercial purposes or worse. We go around like cyborgs, constantly connected and available, inseparable from our cell phones, prostheses that are often literally grafted on to our ears.

Each user creates his or her own personal playlist, as it were on the Internet. He or she interacts and communicates in a personalized and immediate way. Simultaneity also means that an infinite number of programs are broadcast simultaneously. To each their own different content. There is an obvious positive side to the fact that each individual is able to choose the content he or she is most interested in; for example, being able to watch the poetic videos of Pina Bausch's dance performances rather than some horrible talk show. However, there is also the risk of an excessive fragmentation of experience. There are, however, moments when the whole community actually needs to come together in spirit and to be on the same wavelength.

An uninterrupted flow of data reaches us. The invasion of pixels can either enrich us or prevent us from forgetting, and therefore also from thinking. Borges's much-cited "Funes the Memorious" again springs immediately to mind. The instantaneity of information-perception replaces the duration necessary for perception-understanding, which is instead based on a circular temporality, under the banner of Freud's "afterwardness" (*Nachträglichkeit*).

The masses of junk mail and pop-up ads that bombard us every day and rob us of our precious time ironically stand as a metaphor for the trash in the emails we do accept. In no way are they treated as if they were intrusions into our private space (which is in fact what they are) and this is reflected in the compulsion we all feel to check our mail more or less constantly. Curiously, the opposite phenomenon occurs, namely when sometimes work emails fail to reach me because the Mac mail program has automatically classified them as spam.

If I want, I can open several windows at the same time on the computer screen: social networks, mail, push technology for news, TV or streaming movies, YouTube videos, the spreadsheet I'm writing on, music on iTunes, etc. The very names of the applications that make this kind of simultaneous viewing possible are significant. On a Mac they are called Mission Control, Dashboard, Exposé, Launchpad, Spaces, etc. As the online presentation puts it, "see everything at a glance and go everywhere with a click". What's more, Power Nap keeps updating all your data even while you are asleep. In short, the Internet lives and lets you live in the dimension of simultaneity. Its success proves that it meets a need – and you are seduced into satisfying it there and nowhere else. Perhaps that's why it's so addictive.

But what meaning should we give to this need for simultaneity?

Simultaneity

To seek to answer this question, I am drawing inspiration from a wonderful short story by Ingeborg Bachmann written in 1972 (in other words, in the pre-Internet era) titled "Simultan". The title in English is "Word for Word" (published in 1989 by Holmes and Meier in a collection bearing the title *Three Paths to the Lake*). My aim is to look at the psychological meaning of the temporality we are living through in an age dominated ever more by the Internet through the prism of this story. The protagonist of the story is Nadja (a woman's name that in Russian means "hope", but in Spanish is close to the word for "nothing" or "no one" – multilingualism is one of the predominant stylistic hallmarks of this text). With a failed marriage behind her, she has left her home city, Vienna, and her country. She travels around the world, passing from one luxury hotel to another working as a simultaneous interpreter at various important conferences. Told from her point of view, the story is about a trip from Paestum to Maratea in Italy, in the company of a man also from Vienna who works for the FAO in Rome. During the week they spend together, the man gives her back her language. Something moves inside her, and Nadja is forced to think about the deep meaning of her escape into a state of rootlessness (*Heimatlosigkeit:* having no homeland). Words had lost their meaning. Nadja had cancelled herself as a subject. The world was reduced to a babel of languages. However, re-integrating her self is not without pain. A panic attack forces her to face the emptiness she has always sought to escape from.

Nadja realizes that she has deluded herself into thinking that she can deprive herself of her identity or that a fictitious identity is enough. She also realizes both that she has done this because her identity was torn and that she had used her profession to defend herself against the pain of loss.

And yet it was a very arduous activity (clearly there was a price to pay).

The story is told using a stream-of-consciousness style of narration, and Bachmann brings into play several different languages to give a sense of Nadja's segmented experience of reality. Simultaneous translation seen as perfect translation, translation that is faithful, that makes it possible to live without having a single thought, where there are no differences, no slippage or misunderstandings, is the metaphor of the type of temporality which Nadja has immersed herself in and through which she has put in order her experience of things. On the fantasy level, she had kept herself in a state of fusion with the object. Desire coincided with satisfaction. It was a way of obliterating her body as separate from her mother's; the body as signifier is then the body of language and thus what makes it irreducible to meaning. And, with her body, she also erased emotions. But Nadja begins to feel the symptoms of a profound malaise. The man helps her realize that she can actually live and not just pretend to live. The crisis is also an opportunity, a "catastrophic change" (Bion, 1974) through which she will come to take a different view of "translation" or in other words, her life; no longer will it be an automatic and depersonalized activity, but rather the actual re-creation of meaning starting from her own subjectivity and in a new context. She moves from simultaneity viewed as a short circuit in the dialectical dimension of time, waiting and absence, to simultaneity as the ability to see things from multiple points of view that are all active at the same time, in line with the way it is conceived in modern physical sciences. Nadja takes back her existence.

Hallucinosis

Bion (1965, p. 5) writes: "[T]olerance of frustration involves awareness of the presence or absence of objects and of what a developing personality later comes to know as 'time' and (since I have described the 'position' where the breast used to be) 'space'". The way in which we live time and space therefore bears the traces of the most ancient experiences inscribed in the memory of our body (Civitarese, 2019). It is an index of how the process of construction of our subjectivity took place, of how a person inhabited what Julia Kristeva (1974) calls the "semiotic chora", of the quality of their primary relations. A lived sense of time and space is not acquired automatically. For Laplanche the unconscious is formed as a result of the infant's translation of the enigmatic messages that the mother unknowingly sends the child in a situation of radical asymmetry. This is the essence of his theory of generalized seduction. What is untranslatable about these sexualized messages is deposited as a thing representation and becomes the source of the drives. In this way, clinical practice as a whole can be seen from the perspective of the metaphor of translation and the non-biological but inter-human origin of the psychic apparatus. For example, some patients live "in exile" as hypochondriacs (Civitarese, 2011). Others are always afraid of being late. This is why they put their watches forward ten or fifteen minutes. This does not mean that they stop being systematically late. Usually, the ploy proves completely ineffective. Rather, it is a symptom that reveals what the fantasy relationship with the object is made of. It is the relationship with an object experienced as if it always arrived late. In the self, a chasm opens up into which the ego risks falling at every step. The "symptom" of being late serves several purposes: it magically makes the object disappear (it is not encountered in time); it re-enacts the trauma and evacuates one's own anguish into the other. The way in which experiences of time and space are related to each other and originate from the primary relationship with the object becomes an extraordinary model in Bion's description of the transformation in hallucinosis.

Transformation in hallucinosis is a type of denial that occurs both in psychotic patients and in patients who do not have real hallucinations but who live in the concreteness of reality onto which they paste their "hallucinations". These patients are cut off from the living source of their emotional life. Bion hypothesizes that upstream there was a catastrophic experience of explosion or infinitization of the maternal container. The maternal container has expanded to unheard-of dimensions and while continuing to exist – which forces us to theorize denial as an intersubjective fact – it has lost its ability to shape the child's violent emotions. But it also produces dispersal on the level of time. If what gives meaning to things is the presence of a container (of course, these are processes, but let us imagine it as if it were actually a container), if this expands to infinity, it takes an infinite length of time to set up a relationship between two points (events) that are now infinitely distant from one other, something which was easy enough when they were seen side by side. In transformations in hallucinosis, the meaning of things is lost. They are perceived but not really understood. According to Bion, one possesses a consciousness, one registers perceptual data, but one cannot become a conscious or really assimilate these data. One can perceive without understanding or one can perceive *and* understand. But understanding is something given by the breast, as Bion writes in *Cogitations* (1992); and once internalized this is then the alpha function of the mind. Becoming conscious means giving a personal meaning to experience. What does this signify? That we have to dream it. Where there is the dream work, there is symbolization/ understanding (Grotstein, 2000). Dreaming reality is the way we digest the emotions generated by friction with reality. We need reality, but reality is meaningless if it is not tinged with emotions. A reality purified of emotions is arid, "scientific" and inauthentic.

Simultaneity therefore comes from the voiding of space by infinitizing the container – the Net is by definition in a state of infinite expansion – but the same result also occurs when the container collapses and becomes point-like. Here, too, two events previously connected to each other end up coinciding, and likewise they cannot be related, albeit for opposite reasons. The counterpart of an absent object is an object that is excessively present. For example, the overly intelligent mother, that is, the mother who idealizes her role to the point of putting it before the actual needs of the child.[1] This is how we interpreted (Capello & Civitarese, 2010) the futurist glorification of speed and mechanical human at the beginning of the twentieth century – as the expression of a certain manic attitude caused by impossible grief in the face of the collapse of important institutional containers. In some respects, the Internet is the triumphant realization of the futurist dream of "multiplied life" expressed by Fedele Azari in his extraordinary 1927 manifesto "La vita simultanea futurista" (*Simultaneous Futurist Life*).[2] Here is a particularly fascinating passage from this work:

> The exasperating slowness to which we are still condemned despite the apparent achievement of speed (so grotesquely disparaged by diehard lovers of the past) and the desire to prolong our existence by living more and more intensely, lead us to develop simultaneity to the utmost. Indeed, this faculty achieves practically the same results as speed. . . . Trains equipped with telephones, cinema and radio, complicated mechanical armchairs that simultaneously provide hairdressing, manicures, pedicures, massages, the opportunity to listen to the radio and use the telephone, the *dansants variété* diners that enliven the most important cosmopolitan and sophisticated centres, are characteristically modern examples of simultaneous life.

By this point, the interpretation I am putting forward of the pathologies related to the Internet should have become clear: they find in the network the ghost of a maternal object that is unable to contain because it is infinite or because it is all too present and invasive.

Simultaneity *vs.* unison

Is the Internet then just a metaphor for a "technological" functioning of the mind that can completely disregard new information technologies? Does the simultaneity that informs Nadja's life or the simultaneity that seduces us all on the Internet (Google also has an immediate, automatic, mechanical translation function, which sometimes proves useful, but which as soon as the phrasing becomes more complex throws up nonsense translations) bring to the surface something that has always – even before the advent of the Internet – been inside people who suffer from the feeling of living a flat, lifeless existence? In vulnerable subjects, does the temporality that distinguishes new computer communication technologies offer only an easy refuge as a defence against a reality too often perceived as traumatic? Is the Internet the direct cause of new forms of pathology or does it only heighten their expressiveness?

We do not know the answer to these questions. I think it's worth keeping them open. The Internet is a phenomenon of extraordinary complexity, and any evaluation of it cannot be reduced to a few formulae. It is true that from a certain point of view there is nothing new under the sun: the gods of ancient Greece are now the Avengers of Hollywood films; cyborgs are the successors of doubles in romantic literature, etc. However, it is also true that new technologies are particularly invasive. Most importantly, the speed of their introduction has been so rapid as to defy our proverbial adaptability. So, it is safe to say that we are faced with something new and disturbing and also potentially harmful. Having said that, however, for my part I distrust psychoanalysis when it turns into amateur sociology; rather I prefer to see what the new metaphors that technology makes available to us say about our models and methods. This is already a kind of significant repercussion that the Internet has had on our practice. Metaphors are not ornamental or spurious but rather they inspire theory and its clinical application. Elsewhere, for example, I have looked at virtual reality as a way of examining the fictional context in which analysis takes place or the phantasy of immortality expressed in literature and artistic productions inspired by cyborgs (Civitarese, 2010).

So, to look at what we do from the perspective of the Internet, and not vice versa, another question to ask might be: how does the seduction of simultaneity manifest itself in analysis? Some of our patients demand an immediate response, the satisfaction of a need or a desire. Pauses, reflection and periods of waiting are not tolerated. This is perhaps one of the reasons why psychoanalysis is out of sync with a frenetic and constantly "hyper" world. In particular, borderline patients express the need for simultaneity by constantly asking for reassurance. They keep asking questions but do not wait for the answer. Or rather, they want the answer to be simultaneous, so as to instantly cancel out any difference. Furthermore, they are not interested in the content of the answer. They cast it aside immediately. It is evident that the essential communication takes place in the "somatic third" (Rappoport, 2012), and that it only apparently concerns content. For these patients (but in fact for everyone) it is a question of steering them from simultaneity (as pure temporal coincidence) to unison (as keeping the same pace). Simultaneity is fake unison. It implies recognition (identity) but not difference. Simultaneity does not deliver order. Unison, on the other hand, implies a recognition and, since this recognition can never be absolute identification, it always also implies a certain difference. The difference between simultaneity and unison lies in the capacity for reverie and containing the object, which in turn presupposes the existence of an emotional bond.

When it comes to the analyst, on the other hand, simultaneity is played out as the immediate saturation of meaning, such as in clinging to theories (the concept of "grasping"; Ferro, 2009). It can happen with any theory but in my opinion it is more likely in the case of theoretical models that emphasize history and material reality. Giving too much weight to history results in our neglecting the patient's suffering or, rather, it can produce an understanding of it from the outside that is only rational and, in the best-case scenario, through conscious identification. The ever-present risk is that we set up a kind of operative thinking-in-facts and memories-as-facts, producing rationalizations without true affective participation. Moved to pity, analysts defend themselves from their own unconscious and unburden themselves of a large share of responsibility. The distinctive hallmark of psychoanalysis, namely the attention it pays to the unconscious, is lost. The perspective narrows down to history and thus the analyst "perceives" without understanding and "feels" without suffering. What I think is needed to remedy this tendency is receptivity and listening. We need to give centrality to the dream paradigm and to adopt the Freudian notion of unconscious communication between minds in a radical iteration. I would tend to emphasize this formula, which implies the concepts of the analyst's internal setting and style of listening, and not that of the here-and-now, which is sometimes misunderstood as if it called for a sort of absurd and suffocating translation of the patient's discourse that is performed in real time and – the operative word – simultaneously. It would be nothing more than a traumatic re-incorporation of material reality into psychic reality that doesn't help integration. The temporality of analysis is the temporality through which the mind is built. The simultaneity that prevents psychic growth is akin to shutting out doubt and uncertainty and using psychoanalytic theories as a screen to avoid seeing what is there. If the analyst works in the here and now, the analyst becomes the patient's O, to refer one last time to Bion. The analyst who fills his or her head with theories, facts and memories is at most capable of achieving transformations in K (which stands for "knowledge"). The difference is between a Google-analyst, the automatic translator of the truth of the unconscious, and the analyst who indeed translates, but always starting from a reflection on his or her own unavoidable subjectivity.

Notes

1 See Bion (1965, pp. 62–63):

> The mother's inability to accept the projective identifications of the infant and the association of such failure with disturbances in understanding is matched by complications arising through the existence of an extremely understanding mother, particularly understanding by virtue of ability to *accept* projective identification. A reaction associated with this resembles character disorder, an unwillingness to face loss of an idyllic state for a new phase and suppression of the new phase because it involves pain.

2 English translation available at: www.unicamp.br/chaa/rhaa/downloads/Revista%2013%20-%20artigo%208.pdf (Accessed on 20th August 2021).

References

Azari, F. (1927). *La vita simultanea futurista. Direzione del Movimento Futurista.* Milano: A. Taveggia.

Bachmann, I. (1972). Word for word. In: *Three Paths to the Lake* (pp. 1–36). New York and London: Homes & Meier, 1989.

Bion, W.R. (1965). *Transformations: Change from Learning to Growth.* London: Heinemann.

Bion, W.R. (1974). *Il cambiamento catastrofico. La Griglia/Caesura/Seminari brasiliani/Intervista.* Torino: Loescher, 1981.

Bion, W.R. (1992). *Cogitations.* London: Karnac.

Capello, F., & Civitarese, G. (2010). Changing styles, affective continuities and psychic containers: Corrado Govoni's early poetry. *Journal of Romance Studies*, 10:11–25.

Civitarese, G. (2010). Do cyborgs dream? Post-human landscapes in Shinya Tsukamoto's Nightmare Detective (2006). *International Journal of Psychoanalysis*, 91:1005–1016.

Civitarese, G. (2011). L'ipocondria e l'esilio. In: V. Egidi Morpurgo & G. Civitarese (Eds.), *L'ipocondria e il dubbio. L'approccio psicoanalitico* (pp. 105–122). Milano: Franco Angeli.

Civitarese, G. (2019). The concept of time in Bion's "Theory of Thinking". *International Journal of Psychoanalysis*, 100:182-205.

Ferro, A. (2009). Transformations in dreaming and characters in the psychoanalytic field. *International Journal of Psychoanalysis*, 90:209–230.

Grotstein, J. (2000). *Who Is the Dreamer, Who Dreams the Dream? A Study of Psychic Presences*. London: Routledge, 2014.

Kristeva, J. (1974). *Revolution in Poetic Language*. New York: Columbia University Press, 1984.

Rappoport, E. (2012). Creating the umbilical cord: Relational knowing and the somatic third. *Psychoanalytic Dialogues*, 22:375–388.

Chapter XIII

The pleasure of the analytic session

There have been numerous works on the subject of pain in analysis – a feeling that is seen as one of the "elements" of psychoanalysis. One need only think of Bion's assertion that we become what we are capable of suffering. Pain is regarded as the essential ingredient that brings about transformation. Avoiding pain leads to a series of often very costly defences and even to real pathologies. Balzac's novel *The Wild Ass's Skin* warns us of the dangers inherent in avoiding pain. For his part, Pennac (1997, p. 33) reminds us that "Pain is curious. At its most authentic, pain defends itself by crafting sentences". And here we find ourselves midway between narration and narrative transformations as therapy for suffering.

In this context I would like to mention two books by Italian authors: *Un tempo per il dolore* (*A Time for Pain*) by Tonia Cancrini (2002) and *Il dolore dell'analista* (*The Analyst's Pain*) by Maria Adelaide Lupinacci et al. (2015) – two attempts, written several years apart, to take stock of the situation.

My aim in this chapter is to focus on a topic that generally receives little attention: the role of pleasure in analytic work.

Coming as it did not too long after Freud's death, the advent of television in Italy brought with it the phenomenon of adapting famous novels for television. The storylines of these novels were familiar to some but not to the majority. All the viewer had to do to stay ahead of the game was to buy a copy of the novel before watching the upcoming episodes, and in some way the unpredictable could be predicted.

Over a relatively short period of time, in quick succession, *Jane Eyre, Nicholas Nickleby, Crime and Punishment, The Idiot* – I'm going from memory here – and many others appeared on our TV screens and achieved

DOI: 10.4324/9781003279020-13

great success. Some years later, so-called *telefilms* (TV series) came along. Always featuring the same main characters, each episode had a self-sufficient storyline and correspondingly a different cast of secondary characters. These ranged in kind from *Rin Tin Tin* to the German import *Alarm for Cobra 11 – The Highway Police*. Only later did a genre of program emerge that in some ways had its origin in soap operas, or TV serials. Each episode was complete in itself, yet at the same time there was a common thread that developed from one episode to the next.

Nothing was predictable, either within each individual episode or in the series as a whole; moreover, unlike the case of TV adaptations of novels there was no previous text you could consult to know what would happen next; viewers of *ER*, *Sex and the City*, *The Wire*, *The Sopranos*, *The Bridge*, *Homeland*, *The Killing*, *Fortitude*, *House of Cards*, etc. could not know in advance or predict anything about the individual episodes or the overall line of development.

You simply had to be patient and wait for the next episode.

As analysts we are inevitably reminded of the guidance Bion gives in *Clinical Seminars*, namely that in each session we should always give the patient a good reason to come back the next time.

As already mentioned, hitherto the pleasure of analytic work, particularly during the session itself, has been given little consideration.

I was recently asked to do an interview on the question of why so many people are fond of TV cooking shows where more or less famous chefs entertain viewers with recipes, challenges and culinary performances, or act as judges of culinary tournaments. In this case aspiring chefs take the place of Ivanhoe and often come in for a great deal of ill treatment. Clearly there are people who get some kind of pleasure out of this. If so, I think it is the pleasure of giving concrete form to what we do with our mind. We cook, we put something together using what reality provides us with: the "pepper" fact, the "aubergine" fact, the "celery" fact, which we then turn into a new form of food, a *caponata* that is the product of wisdom and experience. But it can also be viewed from the opposite vertex: cooking can be seen as the metaphorization of our mental functioning, often called upon in moments of need to cook emotional foods and various other contributions.

For Lévi-Strauss the transition from raw to cooked marks the dividing line between nature and culture. Bion takes a similar view when he talks of transformations from raw (beta) to cooked (alpha), or, in other words, from raw "O" to a version "clothed in lies" – cooked and made digestible in the form of a dream – that results from being immersed in the boiling hot column 2 on the Grid.

So where does the pleasure lie? Part of it can be traced back to novels published in weekly instalments, often on Sundays, where each episode ended with an unexpected twist, a way of keeping readers on tenterhooks as they waited for the next instalment. It is difficult here not to think of the *Human Comedy*!

But there is something more, what I would call the Fruttero and Lucentini effect – the fact of there being two authors in search of characters to play a part in the analytic narrative. Analyst and patient find themselves acting as two directors who are attempting to turn a scene/dinner (in Italian the word *scena* (*scene*) contains the word *cena* (*dinner*)) into a film, because the unthinkable is in urgent need of "thinkers" – or, as Thomas Ogden would put it, in search of dreamers. Even the most neutral and lacklustre analyst will enter the scene with his or her characteristics. *The analyst cannot avoid being involved in co-narration.*

Another feature is the total unpredictability of the next episode, of which we are co-creators but also co-spectators. Once, when I naively tried to explain to a teenager in analysis what I thought I had understood, his response was to say, "Mr Parmesan is not my type, however good he is. I need fresh milk!".

The transformations we bring about are therefore an essential means of producing pleasure. I have now built on those described by Freud and especially by Bion to include transformations in dreams, transformations in play and transformations in biography. As it happens, we have been carrying out these last kinds of transformation for a long time without being aware of the transformative element that was intrinsic to them.

The narrative transformations Corrao talks about form a bridge linking the various metaphors I have been using so far.

To sum up, we have the pleasure of the story itself (*The Thousand and One Nights*, Proust's *Recherche*, and we could also add Salgari and Verne); the genesis of the characters; the period of waiting for something to develop and come to life, the discovery, the insight, but above all the development of narrative clumps that had previous been under narcosis and that can now come back to life or live for the first time.

The story and the plot

The story: Lucia wants to marry Renzo, Don Rodrigo is against it: "This marriage is not to take place". Many vicissitudes later, the two get married.

The plot: the *Bravi* (thugs), the plague, Don Abbondio, his cousin Attilio, Lodovico and Fra Cristoforo, the Unnamed, Cardinal Federigo, the Nun of Monza, Fra Galdino, Don Ferrante and Donna Prassede, the tailor's house – we could go on endlessly about these characters, who form branches and twigs ramifying off the central narrative trunk.

The story represents the cornerstone of analysis, too, but beauty lies precisely in the way the plot, the characters, the atmospheres and the places (which are also characters) not only embellish the story but make it into something that can be narrated and shared.

What would happen if Botticelli's Primavera or Gilda in the eponymous film were reduced to bare bones or a skeleton? Clearly, Gilda's dance to the tune of *Put the Blame on Me* would turn into a *danse macabre*.

Beauty lies in the creation of semantic and narrative clusters, in the inventiveness of the weaving together of story and narremes that expand and multiply driven by the germinative and creative thrust of the field brought to life by the psychic life of patient and analyst.

Often the story can be summed up in an unconscious fantasy, in a symptom, in the defences that are deployed.

There are a thousand ever-changing facets in the leap towards matters clinical and human involving analyst and patient; this creativity is the driving force, the "beauty" of analysis. Many are afraid of creativity in psychoanalysis because it continually plays havoc with the known.

A colleague was scandalized when I said that I "liked" being an analyst; he felt that this meant I had insufficient regard for suffering and pain (the things we constantly find ourselves engaging with).

To me, however, there is beauty even in the episode involving Cecilia ("Coming down the steps of one of the doorways . . .") or the death of Ivan Ilyich, or the harrowing pages describing the death of Prince Andrei.

Creativity is also capable of opening up, transforming and metabolizing the pain, suffering, agony and ghastliness that make up the mix of being human.

Red Dragon, *The Silence of the Lambs* and Hannibal Lecter are beautiful to read, as are the *Millennium* trilogy or Pirandello and Shakespeare or Dante and Molière, Dumas or Mary Sue, Tolstoy and Dickens.

I deliberately mix together high-brow and low-brow literature because with any given patient we never know which genre awaits us: high, low, heart-wrenching, joyful, painful.

This is the fascinating "mystery" of a session that is always the first, that of an unknown patient, not yesterday's but the us of today with today's him: Sahara, Isis, Swamp, Forests, Pack, Seville, Paris, all places of the group mind or the mind of the field.

We should dare to go to the unknown where "the eagles dare" and where the chicks take refuge: an analytical city without excessive prohibitions of transit and without obligatory senses or prohibitions of access.

Narrative decoration

Francesca

During her analysis Francesca oscillates between three different mental functions. The first is the sense of persecution she feels every time I tell her something. Not that she registers the verbal level of communication, but the very fact of being exposed to the sensoriality of my interventions creates scenes in which the head of the department where she works persecutes her, offends her, imposes his point of view on her (this goes beyond the "violence of interpretation"; it is the violence of the presence and the phonatory act of the Other!).

Suddenly I find myself almost no longer able to speak, which has the effect of alleviating her sense of persecution, except for the occasional minor intervention or exceptional change of setting ("My head physician insults me, presumes he has the right to decide for me; it's a form of abuse").

I don't know how to escape from this narrow, constrained path, but then Francesca finds the solution: she decides to write a detective story. This seems to me to be a brilliant idea, especially when she tells me that she wants to write a book about how to murder her head physician using a seemingly harmless cocktail of drugs and foods. She launches herself into research on the Internet on the interaction between pharmacological substances and ingredients present in foods. This path seems to open a crack in Francesca's persecutory world and to slowly decontaminate it: the patients she sees in the hospital are no longer immuno-depressed (in other words, defenceless) or suffering from AIDS but begin to have working immune systems.

At this point another problem presents itself, a new mental functioning. This more relaxed atmosphere is more conducive to coupling and engenders positive feelings in Francesca. These immediately manifest themselves as "shocking love affairs" which, even if experienced in the here and now, are backdated to episodes that occurred when she was at university or graduate school.

The intimacy is only present on the emotional plane and in her memory there is a fantasy of the occasional kiss, but this is apparently enough to open up horizons of fiery passion. From time to time "he" sends a message that upsets her and keeps her awake at night, prey to unspeakable desires and whirlwinds of emotions.

At this point I intervene, deciding to create space and "narratability" for these states of mind, and this seems to work even without any interpretations (a reverie puts me in contact with a "mediastinal abscess" that, before anything else, needs to be drained). All this leads us to a third line, where emotions doze off, and I am the first to fall victim to this, running the risk of falling "asleep" at each session.

Thus, whereas when she had been awake and was feeling persecuted or in love, she had been unable to conceive a child (also in the sense of new thoughts coming into being in the analysis) to the point where she was considering donor fertilization; now a child has been conceived almost while she was asleep.

Francesca seems to need her own space to be able to generate something.

These spaces of silence are defended both through sleep induction (concoctions to kill the head physician or cause him to die of sleep) and by subduing whirlwinds of passion; but above all by unleashing a barrage of words that evacuate anxiety without communicating anything. I wonder what to do with these outpourings of words that sometimes go on for entire sessions. I decide to wait and let her "evacuate". After a long period of erecting walls constructed out of unstoppable words, Francesca *dreams of giving great quantities of plastic bottles to her sister Nina. Not knowing what she should do with them, Nina tells her that she will set them aside and perhaps turn them into sculptures.* I begin to wonder which characters grouped together in possible forms might enable us to carry on with the narration.

One Monday, Francesca describes how that morning someone had pressed the intercom buzzer to her house, which had made her feel scared. It was a plumber asking for her husband. Worried about this intruder, she had switched off the intercom. All she had understood was that he had brought some mushrooms. Something begins to take shape.

She begins the session the next day by talking about accompanying her 9-month-old son to a cardiologist to have an ECG. However, they couldn't go through with the procedure because he kept on screaming; she must have been terribly afraid.

She then describes a planned home visit to a patient who is so scared she has barricaded herself in. At this point I feel I can start, as it were, "rough-hewing" a statue out of the plastic bottles:

"May I say something?" (interrupting the flow of words).

"Yes, of course!"

"I was wondering if Stefano's screams might possibly resemble your incessant talking about him, with the result that the cardiologist can't do the ECG to find out what's in his heart."

"Well, that's a lot like us . . .".

"And I'd also like to add that there is perhaps another similarity: talking for 50 minutes is a way of keeping me out, of preventing me from coming closer for fear that I might enter your home."

"I find that convincing too: that's how we used to behave at home. We were wary of everyone. My grandmother used to say: one must also be wary of one's intestines, because sometimes they speak during the silence. What's more, we couldn't have friends; everyone was a potential enemy."

"It's easier to understand the story of the plumber and the fear he provoked", especially because of the ambiguity of the gift: was he bringing tasty mushrooms or poisonous toadstools?

Moving on a few months: Francesca begins one session by talking about a patient of hers admitted to hospital with a severe form of delusion. A psychiatrist allegedly gave him a shot while he was sleeping and since then he had lost his mind. Francesca carries on talking about this subject with minimal variations for over half an hour. As soon as she slows down, I step in by asking her if all her non-stop talking is not further evidence of the construction of a wall between her and me that is meant to protect her.

"That makes me think of the patient who is afraid that if he falls asleep, if he lowers his guard, a stream of words might come in through a crack in his attention or in the wall of words that will make him lose his mind. In other words, you are afraid I might say something that makes you feel bad, and so you erect this barrier of words or hypervigilance."

She is quick to acknowledge what I have said, but it is as if she were retreating in flight. So I insist: maybe she agrees with me and runs away so as not to be persecuted by me; perhaps she is behaving like General Kutuzov in *War and Peace* who retreats to safety!

Again, she takes this on board, but with reflective pauses that give me grounds for hoping that some of my interpretative sting has penetrated, but without causing her to lose too much of her mind.

Our world, our field, which previously was only flooded, begins to be decorated with statues, facts, characters and events.

Over a relatively short period we make our way across a depressive wood that seems to paralyze everything; then some new paranoid anxieties appear, and lastly some apparently hypochondriac anxieties that end up in a significant enlargement of the thyroid that does not augur well. Investigations and in-depth analyses are required. There is a nodule with a colloidal extravasation; it could be anything, but more in-depth analyses show that there is a "border" that has a containing function and ensures the benignity of the phenomena. It is true, Francesca tends to indulge in emotional overspill and massive evacuation, but the border has always saved us from any possible flooding.

At moments of emotional outpouring, it is enough for one of the two to say "border", and any excess in danger of overflowing is held in check. So, at this point: "border!"

The field

The analytic field has no limits except those of its constant expansion. Listening in the analytic field is listening through 360 degrees.

In the "space-time" of analysis – which only exists as such in the triad of setting, analyst and patient – there are no off-field phenomena or communications.

Even the most realistic communication is still to be considered relevant to the field despite the fact that some time may be needed to understand its relevance. Each communication will be deconstructed, de-concretized and re-theatricalized through multiple possible scenarios.

In summary

The "Zero Field Time" operation is mourning for Reality.

This Reality corresponds to Zero Time, to "O", to Ultimate (or First) Reality and will be worked through in the Black Hole of column 2 on Bion's Grid (as Grotstein reminds us in such a remarkable way), which opens up like a funnel inhaling "Reality" and transforming it into narration, or going through various stages, by alphabetizing and making it material suitable for the construction of dreams.

The stories will then be embellished and made specific through their arrangement in time and space, and made narratable through the "casting" of characters.

More in full

Go where the patients want us to go with them.

That is to say, from the obsessive Arts Faculty librarian to the bedside of a dying aunt, to the boat show where there are two horrible employers (to use analytic terminology, to be in unison).

Only if the patient feels, and we too feel, comfortable enough in the story can the patient go on freely.

This corresponds to achieving a sufficient degree of harmony so as to make the analytic "multi-sided space" comfortable. In some models this means that the interpretative caesura that can manifest itself in many different ways will come into being (Tuckett et al., 2008).

How to conceive "the characters that enter the session"

At the end of a session Maria reads out a letter to her female analyst: she has written to her ex saying that she wants to save the good things in their relationship and that she will accept his decision that they should split up without rancour.

Communications made during the analytic session operate under a special statute. They are part of "the film that is being co-produced".

Departing from the first movement mentioned, we must bring whatever is available back into the consulting room, back to this shared dramatization; that is to say, we must transform plastic bottles, people, animals, objects, atmospheres into "characters" of the analytic field, resolving not to see them as "presences" belonging to an external reality that is not germane to us as analysts.

A patient who originally came from Brazil begins the session by saying that it was still hot in Brazil and that here it is already cold.

It seems clear to me that the patient has picked up on a difference between her Brazilian emotional temperature and my coldness in the role of "guardian of the setting". If I thought it made sense at that moment, I could make this explicit or I could raise the emotional temperature of the session as a whole or specifically with regard to the act of saying goodbye at the end of it.

If a candidate were to say that he would have appreciated a small "welcome" buffet when he went to his first lesson at the local training institute, I would see this "absence of a buffet" as having entered the current field (we could say that the "buffet or negative buffet" is a character in the field), and this would probably become the organizing principle of the following scenes, or rather of the patient's desire to be welcomed into the session with something that satisfies his thirst and hunger for affection (the buffet).

This raises the usual dilemma as to whether to interpret all this (on the view that this is nutritional in itself) or to make interventions that lead to a +B (positive buffet). The defence mechanisms should be varied and dosed in such a way as to protect us from overly (or extremely) painful anguish. If we overdose a single defence, then the defence becomes more serious than the illness itself.

The Berlin Affair, an extraordinary film by Cavani, provides a wonderful example of where antidepressant keloid defences can lead.

Bearing in mind that O is often unapproachable and unfathomable, although it can in part be made approachable "through lying", that is to say, by running it through the dream column of Bion's Grid, or by dreaming it, one approach is to try to apprehend what different communication segments have in common: nobody listens to me at work, I am taken to task when I put off taking an exam at university, people disapprove when I play music, etc. By eschewing transference interpretations, we are able to pick out the greatest common divisor of the various stories: "As if he sensed the presence of someone who does not listen to him enough and who disparages him".

The TI is made to wear the mask of "someone" (the "masked" or "clothed" TI, that is to say, the Masked Transference Interpretation, passes through defensive border controls more easily because it does not arouse paranoid experiences).

A TI without a mask would be wasted and would produce rejection.

Each interpretation can be tangential or explicit. What the patient says in disorderly fashion can be received by the analyst either from a relational perspective, where the analyst is able to live within the RELATIONSHIP in an interpretive or narrative fashion, or from a FIELD perspective, and in an interpretative manner (but then the field collapses) or narrative manner (where the field contains, narrates, transforms, dreams and plays).

The dream and the stone egg

Luisa dreams *she is inside a landscape reminiscent of* The Shining. *There is snow all around. A taxi is supposed to take her to the gate of a villa; she is a bit scared, she sees buildings with transvestites and prostitutes inside them. She is afraid that the taxi driver will not take her right up to the gate. She is worried about the cold and the atmosphere of suspense.*

I comment that in some way she is experiencing the analysis as a cold, disturbing place where she does not know what to expect; there are only occasional clumps of excitement, but the icy landscape never gets transformed into Mediterranean scrub.

"I'm thinking", she replies, "about the ad for Smart cars. In it there's a montage of shots of someone trying to kill the driver from behind, from the rear seat. Then a voice says: 'Make sure there's no one behind you!'. It's like an anti-ad for analysis. A film with Laura Morante also comes to mind, perhaps *Il Rifugio* or some similar title. A young woman goes to a house where it turns out that something tragic has happened: a terrible child, a monster, used to live in the ventilation ducts, and would steal other people's food. At first, the main character, an enlightened young woman, did not believe this story, but then she came to accept that the house was inhabited by this terrible, now aging ghost. Then I remembered the character played by Jack Nicholson in *The Shining* who had written the same proverb thousands of times: *all work and no play makes Jack a dull boy*. And that's how his wife realized that he was crazy".

"So, analysis is not only a cold and disturbing place, but also a place where a madman constantly repeats the same things, a place that is haunted by terrifying ghosts", I add. "The fact is though", the patient goes on,

"I feel fine here with you. Then the story goes that . . . you always keep a very high temperature".

"Well, I was thinking", I say, "that in my hometown there used to be a cinema, the Smeraldo, with two auditoriums, each showing a different film. If you were in Auditorium A, you could hear the noises coming from Auditorium B and sometimes you could be watching a Bergman film and from 'next door' came the screams punctuating a film about Geronimo or shrieks from a film such as *The Shining* or *Psycho*. I think we must become experts in Auditorium B, the only one that really interests us".

The patient: "In the film I was talking about, there was also a marble egg that fell onto some wooden stairs leaving a mark that was the sign that what had happened was 'true'". To which I add: "It is true that other terrible things happen in Auditorium B. The eggs are made of stone or marble and there is no easy way to fertilize them, but perhaps that is precisely the auditorium that awaits us".

I think that there is one greatest common divisor that joins all these situations, namely, the moment when the alexithymic, concrete aspect, the untransformed beta, rides roughshod over the containment capacity of the container and/or the transformation capacity of the alpha function or of the dream.

This is when the evacuation – whether in the body, in the social body or in the intellect – is too intense for the metabolic-digestive capacity of the mind.

For there to be one symptom or another, what is important are the existential contingencies and the paths that appear more inclined and more conducive to evacuative discharge, whatever the catchment basin. Even there, at times one basin will suffice, at other times it may be like Plitvice, where one lake flows into another and then on into yet another.

These "lakes of beta elements" sometimes spill over from the analytic couch and become life stories.

But there is still something we have to grieve over as therapists: our transformational and containing power is at all events relative and limited.

Of course, the "people" our patients tell us about can only be considered "characters" in the analytic scene or the field. It was necessary to cast these characters in order to be able to dream together the drama of each given patient and to enable their embodiment in a given story. No other characters would have been equally suited. But we need a plot, a deeply felt narrative, to make it a shared dream so that we can treat the trauma that lies behind the story itself. These characters will have to enter and be "baptized" in the reality of the field. Let us look, for example, at the theme of abandonment: it will take concrete form every weekend, every holiday, every end of session, every time there is a breakdown in understanding with the analyst or with the various characters of the camp. There, surrounded by these characters, we will live out a scene in the style of Tarantino, Tavernier, Pasolini or De Sica (father or son). . . . The field will transform, mental states will be given names, new emotions will come to life and be described, new affects, new narrative textures will mould increasingly robust plots to take the place of the void, the hole of abandonment. New and unexpected thoughts will arise where before there had only been a sense of persecution.

Pleasure

I see pleasure in the "narrative capacity" that comes to life in the field through the operations of de-concretization, de-saturation and de-construction that lead to the possibility of co-building, co-narrating, and co-playing.

Reading, writing and playing become the tools and the pillars of creativity.

Starting from saturated and concrete content, we come to weave new emotional experiences.

Ogden put it brilliantly when he stated that that which the patient has not had the opportunity to dream (and transform) becomes a symptom and that this symptom will be dispelled if it is "dreamed" together and woven into a narrative in the analysis.

This operation calls for a taste for enigmas, curiosity, the pleasure of story-telling and, further upstream, reverie and the ability to transform in dream and play.

There are an infinite number of metaphors we could use to describe these processes: going from wool to fabric, from ingredients to a well-cooked dish, from clusters of beta to alpha dreams and night dreams.

Bion (1973–1974) wrote that the patient should always be given a good reason to return: one good reason might be the playing together that relieves anxiety.

When I was a child, I invented a kind of game of battleships using an enormous map of Africa. As things went on, the battle then turned more and more into exploration because the sea only occupied the edges of the map. Many of my classmates would come to play with the electric train (and with the masses of electric wires that gathered under the large table where the tracks ran).

Transforming into images, into links between images, into stories is something truly beautiful. When it works it is like making Russian salad but without the mayonnaise curdling: many heterogeneous ingredients are brought together. Or it is like making a painting by dipping the brush into the palette; or like coming up with a story made up of fragments of sense data.

The pleasure of brain-teasers is more akin to solving puzzles, or discovering things, as in a crossword puzzle or a rebus.

Creative pleasure is connected to the construction and invention of something that was not there before, to the development of functions and abilities – like the evolution of the thumb or the erect position – which open up an infinite number of new possibilities. This is the development of the "filmmaker mind" function, the function performed by the director that starts from the lithotripter of betalomas and ends up in unpredictable narratives.

Alessia

Alessia is a young psychologist who begins analysis because she is required to do so by the school she attends, or so she says. Gradually it will become clear that there are other difficulties and the central figure, the true protagonist of the sessions, will be the violent, abusive brother, who might even be capable of murder.

At first, he is nameless, then a dream captures a face that begins to come into focus. A few months later another dream will see her intent on learning a strange alphabet that appears to unlock experiences and emotions: the fear of dying of a heart attack will become the fear of suffering emotions. The abuses of the brother and stories of stones will turn more into atmospheres and fears than facts; stabs in a dream will become the verbal cruelty of a judge who is a friend of the family playing the part of a grand inquisitor.

A dream will open up blocked paths. *A very dangerous criminal acts under cover of his accent and thus goes unnoticed.* I have a flash of memory: I see children in a primary school class breaking down their names into syllables: E-MA-NUE-LE, A-LES-SIA. As a child in the same class, I am writing an eight horizontally and my mother tells me off: "Wake up that eight, stand him up and tell him not to get the accents wrong!". Alessia was thus able to find a way into the emotional *alexia* (word blindness) that had made it impossible for her to read herself and to read the world.

References

Bion, W.R. (1973–1974). *Brazilian Lectures*. 2 vols. Rio de Janeio: Imago.

Cancrini, T. (2002). *Un tempo per il dolore. Eros, dolore e colpa.* Torino: Boringhieri.

Lupinacci, M.A. et al. (2015). *Il dolore dell'analista.* Roma: Astrolabio, 2015.

Pennac, D. (1997). *Signori bambini.* Milano: Feltrinelli, 2003.

Tuckett, D. et al. (2008). *Psychoanalysis Comparable and Incomparable: The Evolution of a Method to Describe and Compare Psychoanalytic Approaches.* London: Routledge.

Chapter XIV

Aesthetics and writing in psychoanalysis[1]

Reflecting on the failure of his analysis of Dora, Freud asks himself the question:

> Could I have perhaps kept the girl under my treatment. . . . if I had . . . shown a warm personal interest in her, a course which, even after allowing for my position as her physician, would have been tantamount to providing her with a substitute for the affection she longed for?
>
> (1905, p. 109)

And he concludes: "I promised to forgive her for having deprived me of the satisfaction of affording her a far more radical cure for her troubles" (*ibid.*, p. 122). It is now clear that Freud's coldness is to be explained above all on the theoretical level, where the discussion is about the concepts of neutrality and abstinence that are central to classic psychoanalytic theory. Freud still moves within the historical-naturalistic or archaeological-circumstantial paradigm, whereas we are drawing close to an aesthetic paradigm (Civitarese, 2014, 2017).

What does this mean? It means that we are increasingly coming to realize how important the model of the aesthetic and intersubjective constitution of the infant's psyche is for psychoanalytic theory; that the body "thinks", so to speak; that emotions always have to do with relationships and contribute powerfully to making sense of experience and lending thrust and direction to action; and lastly, that we must bear all of this in mind when thinking about therapeutic action. We can no longer neglect, for example, the role of the analyst's personality, her subjectivity, her way of reading the world in ways that cannot be perfectly expressed in concepts. The so-called non-specific factors of treatment – those not attributable to

DOI: 10.4324/9781003279020-14

intellectual understanding and not directly translatable into verbal interpretations – come together in aspects of style. In the various spheres of
psychoanalytic discourse, that is to say, in clinical practice, supervision
and writing, what the analyst expresses is his or her signature, the most
intimate expression of self.

Although this change may seem to undermine the "science" of metapsychology or, rather, psychoanalysis's claims to constitute a positive body
of knowledge of the unconscious processes of the mind, psychoanalysis
nevertheless remains the discipline that possesses the most refined tools
to conceptualize these semiotic, musical, pre-reflective, "poetic" aspects
of communication and relationship – not only effects of signification but
also of sense.

The aesthetic element in the clinical practice of psychoanalysis

To clarify the opposition between sense and signification, let me quote
from Jean-Luc Nancy's book *Listening*:

> *To say* is not always, or only, to speak, or else to speak is not only to
> signify, but it is also, always, to dictate, *dictare*, that is, at once to give
> saying its *tone*, or its *style* (its tonality, its color, its allure) and for that
> or in that, in that operation or in that *tenseness* of saying, *reciting* it,
> reciting it *to oneself* or letting itself recite *itself* – make itself sonorous,
> de-claim itself or ex-claim itself, and cite itself (set itself in motion,
> call itself, according to the first meaning of the word, incite itself),
> send back to its own echo and, by doing so, make itself.
>
> (2002, p. 35, emphasis in original)

There are perhaps no more haunting images to express this concept of the
centrality of the aesthetic element in analysis than the scene in Bergman's
Cries and Whispers, which Petrella recently shared with colleagues at a
psychoanalytic conference in Pavia. The scene features two sisters who,
after many bitter quarrels, silences and misunderstandings, finally manage
to talk to each other passionately, but we don't hear what they are saying. Bergman replaces the words with the sarabande from Bach's cello
suite No. 5. This is precisely the essence of any analytic conversation.

The challenge for contemporary psychoanalysis is to learn how to grasp this essence conceptually and to translate it into guidelines for technique. Affording us another of his incredible insights, Winnicott (1975, p. 184) comes up with an intuition similar to Bergman's to explain why music captures the rhythm of being even ahead of the visuality of painting:

> Belonging to this feeling of impotence [at birth] is the intolerable nature of experiencing something without any knowledge whatever of when it will end. . . . It is for this reason fundamentally that form in music is so important. Through form, the end is in sight from the beginning.

Style, therefore, is a zero-degree method to contain anguish.

It should be clear from this that equating analysis with aesthetic experience is not to be understood as making reference to the merely ornamental aspect of analysis, to the artistic nature of certain dream scenarios and certain discursive constructions, nor does it mean describing in elegant terms something that has little or nothing to do with an artistic experience. On the contrary, aesthetic experience is, in a strong sense, the deepest element of psychoanalysis; it is "central to the constitution both of the mind and of meaning in the analytic situation. The psychoanalytic experience is fundamentally an aesthetic experience" (Barale, 2011, p. 189).

This is the reason why it is so important to take into account the sphere of aesthetics in order to engineer ever more flexible and precise models in psychoanalysis. Likewise, it is crucial to overcome, in both theory and practice, the dichotomy, which began with Freud, between psychoanalysis as a hermeneutics of interpretation and psychoanalysis as an aesthetics of reception; between a psychoanalysis of memories and content on the one hand, and one of transformations and psychic containers, on the other.

This conviction of mine also stems from the view that sense has a radically aesthetic (and largely pre-representative) matrix, as do the "transformative operations which occur and which we attempt to steer in the analytic field, including that thrust towards thinkability, mentalization, and representability that we seek to develop in the field". The aesthetic moment predominates over the merely cognitive moment because it accounts for the patient's tolerability of what appears to the analyst as true in an abstract or conceptual sense. If I focus on the processes of psychic growth more than on content, I do so because I think that the patient will then be able to access repressed contents even more easily; if, on the other hand, I reveal to the patient supposedly repressed contents without taking into account their emotional tolerability – and here I am thinking of the concept of unison *as another level of truth* – this may cause needless wounds.

To use a banal metaphor, I could say that it's possible to love Dylan's songs without knowing the lyrics, but not the other way around. However, for some people the most difficult thing seems to be to realize that *there is always a text*: for human beings, immersed in the symbolic from before birth, as Lacan (1966) says, no emotional exchange takes place that does not presuppose that upstream at least one of the two members of the pair has the basic ability to conceptualize that makes self-awareness possible.

In particular, Bion's psychoanalytic theory (likewise those of Meltzer, Ferro, Ogden, etc.) can be termed "aesthetic" because it puts emotions/ sensations, the αἴσθησις, at the centre of thought, in that it is a radically intersubjective or social form of knowledge of reality. This modality is primary not only in terms of genetics – hence the importance given to the concept of unison – but also because it forms the basis of the authentic feeling of existing throughout life. Furthermore, Bion's theory is also aesthetic because it brings thought back to its anchorage in dreaming, to the operations Freud identified as active in the composition of the explicit text of the dream and also implicated in the dream of artistic creation. Meltzer's concept of aesthetic conflict also develops its full heuristic potential only if it is seen in terms of Bion's original "aesthetic" idea that inspired it: "In the beginning was the aesthetic object and the aesthetic object was the breast and breast was the world" (Meltzer, 1986, p. 204).

Freud perhaps expressed a similar intuition in one of his last notes (dated July 12, 1938), where he wrote that, in a child, being precedes having and that the primordial mechanism of possession is identification: "I am the breast" (*ich bin die Brust*), that is, the object (Freud, 1938, p. 299); it is only later that the consciousness of having, which implies a separation, appears: "I have it, that is, I am not it" (*ich habe sie, d.h. ich bin sie nicht*; *ibid.*). With its compelling concision, this formulation seems once again to emphasize the identity of Ego and body. What is more, it also implies that the Ego is the Other, culture, sociality, essentially a "we", and that the first Ego is a sensorial-affective Ego.

The aesthetic element in psychoanalytic writing

Thus it is all the more necessary to take into account the effects of style – significantly defined by Barthes (2003) as a practice of nuance – even where they are at home, so to speak, that is to say, when the analyst writes. Writing, argues Nancy (2002, p. 35),

> is nothing other than making sense resound beyond signification, or beyond itself. It is vocalizing a sense that, for classical thought, intended to remain deaf and mute, an understanding [*entente*] untimbred [*détimbree*] of self in the silence of a consonant without resonance.

By the same token, in his *ABC of Reading*, Ezra Pound (1934, p. 36) notes: "Dichten = condensare [condensing]". *Dichter* in German means poet. And "to condense", which he writes in Italian, as we know, is what dream work does (in addition to "displacing"). In short, we have outlined a path that places the emphasis on the similarities between the spoken and the written language and, in terms of *dictare*, of both with poetry and dreams. Intrinsic to these forms of expression is the pre-eminence of sense (which is always multifarious, open and vital) over meaning (which tends rather towards closure and stagnation); ambiguity over logical precision; the trait of language that Meltzer (1983) characterizes as song-and-dance over the abstraction of the concept; the "artistic" over the rational element. What does "artistic" mean here? In Bion (1965, p. 32) we read:

> The artist is used here as a model intended to indicate that the criteria for a psychoanalytic paper are that it should stimulate in the reader the emotional experience that the writer intends, that its power to stimulate should be durable and that the emotional experience thus stimulated should be an accurate representation of the psychoanalytic experience (O) that stimulated the writer in the first place.

Freud is already in some respects aware of this artistic element of writing in psychoanalysis, but he takes a totally negative view of it. In some of the passages on Dora he takes head on the question of the nature of his writing as a literary product, and to avoid any misunderstanding he writes:

I am aware that – in this city, at least – there are many physicians who (revolting though it may seem) choose to read a case history of this kind not as a contribution to the psychopathology of the neuroses, but as a *roman à clef* designed for their private delectation.

(1905, p. 9)

What is striking about this passage is precisely Freud's dismissal, expressed using the surprising adjective "revolting", of the style or literary aspect of the text.

Elsewhere Freud makes it clear that essentially his account of Dora's case faithfully reflects how things happened. In doing so, however, he causes a second fracture in the positivistic approach of his discourse by conceding that unassailable fidelity is neither possible nor necessary: "Thus the record is not absolutely – phonographically – exact, but it can claim to possess a high degree of trustworthiness. Nothing of any importance has been altered" (*ibid.*, p. 10). A similar clarification comes later on in the text: "I shall present the material produced during the analysis of this dream in the somewhat haphazard order in which it recurs to my mind" (*ibid.*, p. 95). Later, another remark clearly reveals both what he thinks his position should be – that of an impassive doctor and certainly not a writer – and, equally plainly, his doubts about it: "if I were a man of letters engaged upon the creation of a mental state like this for a short story, instead of being a medical man engaged upon its dissection" (*ibid.*, p. 59), etc. The annotation is significant because it encapsulates Freud's secret worry: what would happen "if I were a man of letters . . ."?

However, what in Freud's eyes may have appeared a defect takes on a completely different meaning for us, because it now seems to us an ineradicable, essential and by no means marginal dimension of expression in psychoanalysis both in clinical practice and in the practice of writing. Ever since the so-called linguistic or rhetorical turning point, we have become well aware of the state of crisis of any strong concept of "truth". Freud's concerns can be read today as an anticipation of current developments in psychoanalysis. He himself laid the foundations for these developments by elevating the systematic deconstruction of logical-rational discourse to the level of a method. Even Bion, once he had been forced to come to terms with an altered epistemological horizon, obsessively questioned himself about what we should consider a fact in analysis, how to account for it to the patient and possibly the reader of an essay with adequate "transformations in writing", about how to use intuition in a mannerly and disciplined fashion. Echoes of his concern to develop this area of psychoanalytic theory are scattered throughout much of his work, oscillating constantly between references to clinical practice and to writing. Here I shall only mention three such places: the first is found in *Transformations* (Bion, 1965), the second in the Paris seminar (Bion, 1978) and the third in "Evidence" (Bion, 1976).

At a certain point in *Transformations* Bion (1965, p. 20) inserts a clinical vignette, and then asks himself what kind of transformation it represents in relation to how things went in the session and to what extent it depicts them truthfully:

> The short report is verbally nearly correct; yet as I read it again I see it is a misleading record of the experience. I shall therefore make another attempt to describe this fragment of session but without attempting verbal exactitude.

Bion goes on to give a second more elaborate version of the same scene that is less consistent with the principle of "verbal exactitude", and is therefore "misleading". And yet he considers the second version more "true" than the first. How is this possible? Because nothing, he argues, is more fallacious than a mechanical record. Indeed, any mechanical recording will necessarily exclude imaginative and affective understanding, which can only be supplied by an effective "fiction"; hence the need to take the artist as a model. To get a clearer idea of what Bion means, let us read a fragment from each of the two vignettes.

In the first, patient B speaks: "Good morning, good morning, good morning. It must mean afternoon really. I don't expect anything can be expected today; this morning, I mean. This afternoon. It must be some kind of joke" (Bion, 1965, p. 20). The second version describes the same event but reads:

> After his pause of uncertainty, he whispered his good mornings as if he were preoccupied with an object he had lost, but expected to find close at hand. He corrected himself in a tone that might imply a mental aberration that led him to think it "good morning". The speaker of the words "good morning," I gathered, was not really the patient, but

someone whose manner he caricatured. Then came the comment that nothing could be expected. That was clear enough; but who was making the comment, or of whom nothing could be expected, was obscure. It might have been myself; I did not think it was he. Then he spoke of the joke. The way this term was used implied that the joke had no tincture of humour about it. To me it could mean a cruel joke, but such an interpretation depended on an assumption that the words retained the meaning that they would have in sane conversation and that the emotion expressed, by and with them, had the value that it would have in ordinary speech.

(ibid., p. 20)

In this second version, what strikes the reader is the greater number of inferences Bion allows himself to draw and how much more sophisticated the text is in terms of its formal or "literary" elaboration. In addition, there is a more theoretical aspect to consider in relation to the literary character of psychoanalytic writings. It is frequently pointed out that one of the unscientific traits of psychoanalysis is the fact that no author is ever "surpassed". I think this can be explained by the fact that each great author in psychoanalysis (Freud, Klein, Bion, Winnicott, Searles, etc.) creates a world. Having to give an account of such a complex object as the mind, we realize that stylistic features are just as essential as more theoretical ones. We need only think of the kind of ethos that Freud transmits in his writings and that never ceases to move us. Or again, when we re-read a few lines by Klein describing the horror world she "invented" to represent the most archaic and primitive forms of psychic life, we continue to be enthralled. Or we can even think of the sense of peace and wonder that emanates from Winnicott's pages when he uses everyday language to craft poetic formulas that can either be incredibly courageous and unsettling or delightfully provocative. And yet he presents them calmly and with an intimate feeling of assuredness. To take a few examples: it is obvious that the mother must hate the child; there is no child (unless seen together with the mother); from reading Freud's letters to his fiancée we understand that Freud is human; the child also loves separating from the thumb; teenagers play with the things of the world, and so on. *These authors express views of the world and of the essence of humanity that may differ from each other but are all invaluable.*

If we did not grant this point, it would be like saying that Rilke "surpasses" D'Annunzio or vice versa. But even here, even where the levels involved are more stylistic and poetic rather than just theoretical, we know that there is certainly no loss of a sufficient degree of consensuality. Besides, it is no coincidence that Heidegger, the greatest philosopher of the last century, should have looked to poetry as the highest possible expression of human knowledge vis-à-vis the meaning of existence. Of course, given the responsibility they bear and the hybrid nature of their discipline, analysts cannot content themselves with the artistic element; they must also take into account medical and neurological theories, empirical research, etc. However, in my opinion, the greatest risk psychoanalysis runs is that it will progressively lose its real ability to listen to the discourse of the unconscious and transform itself into some spurious form of cognitivistic practice, becoming strangely deaf to the aesthetic aspects of relationship.

The analyst as artist

In his Paris seminar, but also in many other parts of his work, Bion (1978) often turns to the metaphor of the artist. Analysts, he says, should realize how important it is to be sensitive to the artistic aspects of their work. A patient tells him that if he had a piano he might be able to make him understand what he really feels. Bion seems to take seriously the idea of a "musical" instrument also as the medium for the analyst's communication. Obviously we cannot expect everyone to have special, out-of-the-ordinary qualities; however, we can theorize what normal artistic ability might mean.

The whole Paris seminar revolves around the problem of how to transform invisible emotions (not yet transformed, beta emotions) into alpha emotions that can be painted, smelt, tasted, touched. Colours, senses, emotions, desires: this is the lexicon of experience that is alive. Patients come for analysis either because they feel nothing, meaning that they are cut off from the lifeblood of their existence, or because they are shaken by excessively violent emotions that leave them stunned at every occasion. In both cases they are unable to give personal meaning to what happens to them. The truth of their existence escapes them. This is no "scientific" or rational truth but rather an emotional one. However, the truth about the patient that the analyst can offer will only give the patient a sense of joy and fullness of life if it is the result of sharing, only if it comes from some intimate agreement (unison could be viewed as the birth of a primordial concept, a simultaneous experience of unity and multiplicity). The constant problem the analyst faces is how to achieve this truth and how to say it – which is in fact the same thing.

If the analyst wants to say something true and, as Rimbaud (1871) says in his letter to Paul Demeny, to find a language "of the soul, for the soul", like the poet the analyst must become a "seer". Artists are masters of such transformations. Every authentic artist tells the truth, but in their own way, with their own unmistakable style. Take Cézanne, for example (since Bion mentions his paintings of Mont Sainte-Victoire): how does he do it? It's a mystery. Visiting a recent exhibition of Cezanne's works in Milan, at some point I had a kind of (semi-comic) epiphany: ah, that's how he does it! The apples painted on the canvas do not stand still but move! Seeing is believing. They move! This was a way of understanding Cézanne and containing the anxiety of not understanding.

Also in analysis – and when writing – the characters must "move" (they must move us), they must live, they must make an impression on us as if they were made not of paper but of flesh. In "A Paris Seminar" Bion (1978) asks the audience rhetorically if the last scientific article they read in *The International Journal of Psychoanalysis* reminded them of real people. How many articles, books (how many analyses) are stillborn or struggle to find an ounce of vitality? Here we see how the problem of language, expression and writing runs through the whole of psychoanalysis and how wrong it is to imagine a gap between clinical and theoretical activity. Just like communications addressed to the patient, writing should not be depersonalized. Otherwise it would be impossible to convey the deep, affective, semiotic or musical understanding we have of things. The problem, in the session as on the page, is how to transform experience into something that has the flavour of being alive and thus rich in personal meaning.

Finally, to conclude, I would like to mention one of Bion's last articles, "Evidence". This paper came out only shortly before his death and represents a kind of testament. It is a dramatic piece of writing because it tells of the failure of an analysis – similar to Winnicott's (1974) *Fear of Breakdown*, which can be considered his last essay and legacy, where he too speaks of a patient's suicide. It seemed that everything was going well, that the analyst was understanding enough of what was happening. But one day the patient went back to his house and took his own life. What, Bion wonders, had he failed to understand about him? Which "subthalamic" fears – that is, fears perhaps emerging from archaic periods of his life, and therefore, literally, "ineffable" – had he been insufficiently receptive to? It is clear how this extraordinary text tightly interweaves the theme of the aesthetics of the analyst's receptivity with that of primitive or "inaccessible" states of the mind.

To repeat: I would not wish for this need for an analysis of the artistic, poetic or musical element to be confused with the possible use of vaguely aestheticizing expressive registers. The real question is different: how to be effectively communicative both in the writing that is the word and in the writing that is actually written. Here I am using the term *writing* in the sense intended by Derrida (1967) in *Grammatology*, when he puts forward the paradoxical thesis that it *precedes* the word; in other words, its role is to highlight the differential structure of language and the game of signifiers. Above all, the question is how to come as close as possible to a somato-psychic understanding and how to develop a personal "language of achievement" that satisfies the principle of unity of experience.

So what could be meant by the analyst's normal artistic ability, that is to say, the ability to develop sensitivity (also) to the effects of style? Where might the analyst find the colour palette to paint these pictures? Bion's answer is simple: in dreams, "the predominantly unconscious psychological work that we do in the course of dreaming . . . [is the] most encompassing, penetrating, and creative form of thinking" of which human beings are capable (Ogden, 2010, pp. 328). If the analyst is able to make himself or herself receptive to dream thought, the analyst has everything necessary for a poetic or creatively ambiguous and stylistically "accurate" rendering of the experience. The adjective "ambiguous" here means that such a representation activates multiple perspectives; the contradictions are not cancelled out, but rather they enrich the dialectical view one has of the world and of oneself. This occurs by virtue of the peculiar unsaturated quality of dream language, a quality connected to images and the deconstruction of logical discourse.

In my opinion, one of the reasons why the discourse of the unconscious (which Lacan unsurprisingly describes as a language) makes us feel more true and real (Ogden) is because it reunites us with the social background of our identity that can only be inscribed in language. Language is a repertoire of infinite iterations of meaning. It is as if we were constantly called upon to "claim" as much as possible in order to become more human; in other words, it is as if we needed to adopt as many shared and not arbitrary perspectives as possible on the things of the world – which does not exclude conflict or difference. Indeed, as Hegel teaches us, recognition is essentially conflict (dialectic). Events of this kind are manifested in analysis every time the discourse shows signs of coming apart, disharmony, disjunctions or surprising hallucinoses. Re-dreamed (re-claimed) in the emotional immediacy of the encounter, in a fertile conjunction of sociality and individuation, these effects open the way to a plural meaning and help the mind grow.

Conversely, one way of searching for a "musical" chord, a fundamental affective resonance that represents almost a "primordial concept", an affective "we" (Krueger, 2016), a unity between multiple terms, lies not so much in "interpreting" as in talking-as-dreaming (Ogden, 2008), a type of conversation where ample space is reserved for ellipsis and reticence, two figures of silence, but of a silence that is intended to be hospitable. As Heidegger (1981, p. 22) writes in his book on Hölderlin, interpretation should be like snow that falls and then disappears without a trace: "The last, but also the most difficult, step of every interpretation consists in its disappearing".

If we transpose this need into the field of psychoanalysis, what, let us ask ourselves, should ideally "disappear"? I believe this to mean anything about the style of listening and expression that weighs down and hinders communication instead of enhancing it, and that deprives the patient of the possibility of doing their own personal processing work. It is better, therefore, to converse than to interpret; to use an everyday verbal register; but above all to "force oneself" to intuit what is happening by bringing our psychoanalytic listening to the unconscious up to the level of highest sensitivity.

This is what happens in the post-Bionian model of the analytic field. The analyst focuses on the unconscious communication that takes place in the here and now. Thus, the analyst adheres to a phenomenological criterion of "immediacy" – which is followed in various ways and with various results by all psychoanalytic models (Civitarese, 2016) and whose motto could be borrowed from Husserl (1900, p. 168), who writes in his *Logical Investigations*: "We must go back to 'things themselves'". Obviously, he takes into account the patient's biography and concrete reality, but keeps them in the background. Rather, in order to intuit what deep emotional experience (O) is involved at any given moment – for Bion the only thing that matters in analysis – he subjects them to a kind of centripetal effect: he sees virtually everything as an element in the analytic field and the dream of the session. When this happens, he instantly feels *emotionally* more responsible and involved, and can more easily fuse intellectual and affective ("bodily") understanding. As is clear to see, even if they are two different sides to the same coin, what is important is that the *"artistic" aspect resides at the pole of receptivity rather than the pole of expression.*

Note

1 Paper read at the conference organized by the Psychoanalytic Centre of Florence: "Writing psychoanalysis: scientific, ethical and cultural implications". Pisa, Scuola Normale Superiore, 13 February 2016.

References

Barale, F. (2011). Postfazione. Griglie e grisaglie. In: G. Civitarese (Ed.), *La violenza delle emozioni. Bion e la psicoanalisi post-bioniana.* Milano: Raffaello Cortina.

Barthes, R. (2003). *The Preparation of the Novel: Lecture Courses and Seminars at the Collège de France (1978–1979 and 1979–1980).* New York: Columbia University Press.

Bion, W.R. (1965). *Transformations: Change from Learning to Growth.* London: Heinemann.

Bion, W.R. (1976). Evidence. In: *Clinical Seminars and Other Works* (pp. 312–320). London: Karnac, 2008.

Bion, W.R. (1978). A Paris seminar. In: C. Mawson (Ed.), *The Complete Works of W.R. Bion* (Vol. IX). London: Karnac, 2014.

Civitarese, G. (2014). *Truth and the Unconscious.* London: Routledge, 2016.

Civitarese, G. (2016). Truth as immediacy and unison: A new common ground in psychoanalysis? Commentary on essays addressing "Is truth relevant?" *Psychoanalytic Quarterly*, 85, 449–501.

Civitarese, G. (2017). *Sublime Subjects: Aesthetic Experience and Intersubjectivity in Psychoanalysis.* London: Routledge.

Civitarese, G. (2019). The concept of time in Bion's "A Theory of Thinking". *International Journal of Psychoanalysis* 100:182-205

Derrida, J. (1967). *Of Grammatology.* Baltimore, MA: Johns Hopkins, 2016.

Freud, S. (1905). Fragment of an analysis of a case of hysteria (1905 [1901]). *SEW*, 7:1–122.

Freud, S. (1938). Findings, ideas, problems. *SE,* 23:299–300.

Heidegger, M. (1981). *Elucidations of Hölderlin's Poetry* (M. Heidegger, Ed.) (p. 22). New York: Humanity Books, 2000.

Husserl, E. (1900/1901). *Logical Investigations, Volume 1* (J.N. Findlay, Trans.). London: Routledge, 2001.

Krueger, J. (2016). The affective 'we'. Self-regulations and shared emotions. In: T. Szanto & D. Moran (Eds.), *Phenomenology of Sociality*. London: Routledge.

Lacan, J. (1966). *Écrits, First Complete Edition in English*. New York: W. W. Norton & Company, 2006. (Original work published 1966)

Meltzer, D. (1983). Dream-life: A re-examination of the psychoanalytic theory and technique. *Dream-Life: A Re-Examination of the Psychoanalytic Theory and Technique*, 142:1–185.

Meltzer, D. (1986). *Studies in Extended Metapsychology: Clinical Applications of Bion's Ideas*. London: Karnac.

Nancy, J-L. (2002). *Listening*. New York: Fordham University Press, 2007.

Ogden, T.H. (2008). On talking as dreaming. *International Journal of Psychoanalysis*, 88(3):575–589.

Ogden, T.H. (2010). On three forms of thinking: Magical thinking, dream thinking, and transformative thinking. *Psychoanalytic Quarterly*, 79(2):317–347.

Pound, E. (1934). *ABC of Reading*. New York: New Directions, 2010.

Rimbaud, A. (1871). Letter to Paul Demeny. In: *Rimbaud: Complete Works, Selected Letters, a Bilingual Edition*. Chicago: University of Chicago Press, Revised edition, 2005.

Winnicott, D.W. (1974 [1963]). Fear of breakdown. *International Review of Psycho-Analysis*, 1:103–107.

Winnicott, D.W. (1975). Through pediatrics to psycho-analysis. *International Psycho-Analysis Library*, 100:1–325. London: The Hogarth Press and the Institute of Psycho-Analysis.

Editorial notes

Chapter II is based on: Civitarese, G. (2018). Vitality as a theoretical and technical parameter in psychoanalysis. *Romanian Journal of Psychoanalysis*, 11:121–138.

Chapter III is based on: Ferro, A. (2018). Attacks on linking, or uncontainability of beta elements? In: C. Bronstein and E. O'Shaughnessy (Eds.), *"Attacks on Linking" Revisited: A New Look at Bion's Classical Work* (pp. 161–178). London: Routledge.

Chapter IV is based on: Civitarese, G. (2019) The birth of the psyche and intercorporeity. *Fort Da*, 25:6–25.

Chapter VII is based on Ferro, A. (2016). *Freud's "Formulations on the Two Principles of Mental Functioning": Its Roots and Development* (pp. 129–147). In Brown, L. (Ed.) *On Freud's "Formulations on the Two Principles of Mental Functioning"*. London: Routledge.

Chapter VIII is based on: Civitarese, G. (2011). Towards an ethics of responsibility. *International Forum of Psychoanalysis*, 20:108–112.

Chapter X is based on: Civitarese, G. (2010). Le parentesi di Ogden ovvero della continuità dell'esperienza cosciente e inconscia. *Rivista di Psicoanalisi*, 57:763–770.

Chapter XII is based on: Civitarese, G. (2012). Internet e la vita simultanea. *Quaderni de Gli Argonauti*, 24:33–44.

Chapter XIV is based on: Civitarese, G. (2017). Estetica e scrittura in psicoanalisi. *Rivista di Psicoanalisi*, 53:181–193.

Index

♂♀ *see* container/contained (♂♀)